Energy Politics

Energy Politics

Brenda Shaffer

PENN

University of Pennsylvania Press

Philadelphia

Published by
University of Pennsylvania Press
Philadelphia, Pennsylvania 19104-4112

Printed in the United States of America on acid-free paper
10 9 8 7 6 5 4 3 2 1

A Cataloging-in-Publication record is available from the Library of Congress
ISBN 978-0-8122-4200-3

Contents

Introduction

It is not uncommon to hear leaders and states criticized for "mixing oil and politics." Indeed, a standard criticism of the U.S.-led war in Iraq is "it is just about oil." In assessing the merit of various pipeline and energy production projects, companies and governments are warned to stick to "commercial considerations." A 2003 joint United Nations Development Programme (UNDP)/World Bank report on cross-border oil and gas pipelines proposed as one of its main recommendations that projects should be "driven by commercial considerations."[1] The United States and Europe have warned Russia and other energy exporting states to separate energy from their foreign relations. German foreign minister Walter Steinmeier warned that "Energy must not become the currency of power in international politics."[2] U.S. vice president Dick Cheney, referring to Moscow's behavior in its energy trade with its neighbors, noted that "No legitimate interest is served when oil and gas become tools of intimidation or blackmail, either by supply manipulation or attempts to monopolize transportation."[3] Clearly, when exporters overtly use energy exports as a tool to promote their foreign policy goals, Europe and the United States regularly decry the use of energy as a "weapon" rather than accept it as a standard and legitimate tool of foreign policy.

This book claims otherwise: energy and politics are intrinsically interlinked. A country's ability to access energy supplies and the ways in which it uses energy crucially determine the state of its economy, its national security, and the quality and sustainability of its environment. The prevailing lifestyle and structure of global society today is that of "hydrocarbon man"—and the way hydrocarbon man produces goods, wages war, and even finds entertainment is dependent on regular access to fossil fuels. Moreover, for energy exporters and important energy-transit states, energy supply policy is as much a part of the policy arsenal as other economic tools, military power, and diplomatic tactics. States are no more likely to refrain from using energy to promote their policy goals than to ignore economic or military means of doing so. These states have particular leverage in a tight world oil market, since oil prices are especially sensitive to political developments.

Oil prices can also be affected by domestic developments as well as intentional foreign policy strategies. For example, political revolutions, even if they do not harm any individuals or cause sustained damage to production or export, often lead to oil price spikes with international economic ramifications. In fact, political factors significantly affect the commercial viability of energy production and infrastructure projects. One of the major components of the cost of a project can be compensating for the perceived risk. A regime's political orientation and stability, how likely it is to respect signed contracts, and its propensity to become embroiled in regional conflict are all inherently political factors that significantly impact the price tag and perceived worthiness of an energy project.

In addition, infrastructure projects link states and reflect relations. Thus, states in choosing routes to export their commodities and import their energy supplies naturally consider and promote the political ramifications of various route options. Decisions on natural gas export projects are especially likely to be affected by political considerations because they can be quite risky. Investors have to wait a long time before receiving a return on their investment, and such projects involve immense sunk costs. Yet once construction begins, investors have little leverage vis-à-vis the host state. Not surprisingly, regime stability and orientation play a paramount role in deciding where to develop natural gas projects. Indeed, there are interesting examples of neighboring states, such as Iran and Qatar, that sit on common natural gas fields, yet one has succeeded in developing its resources and the other has not.

The growing perception of climate change as a potential security threat to states around the globe has also helped turn energy use policy into a major foreign policy and even national security issue. Politics likewise influences the realm of decisions about what energy-related scientific research to pursue. As will be seen in the case of U.S. energy policy, which nonfossil fuels development receives government funding is largely determined by domestic political considerations, such as winning the support of corn-growing states by encouraging development of corn-based ethanol. In addition, energy policies require trade-offs—for example, nuclear energy may be useful to combat climate change but may spur nuclear weapons proliferation—whose resolution is found mainly in politics.

In the drive to let commercial considerations have the larger role in determining energy policy outcomes, the United States and Europe in the last couple of decades have undertaken a process of rapid privatization and separation of their energy production, transport, and distribution infrastructure. However, these states are discovering that while the market can provide energy supplies, it does not create energy security. Energy security is comprised of three elements: reliability of supply, affordability of resources, and friendliness to the environment. Environmental friendliness and security of supply are not provided by the market. This means that the state will need to stay involved in crafting energy security policies. The market does not create the diverse sources, infrastructures, or storage policies that can enhance security of supply. The market does not know how to fashion wider political relations in a way to foil use of the energy weapon. In addition, the market can lead to decisions to promote short-term personal interests and not the long-term energy security of the state. Moreover, market forces are not really at play in most cases, since, on the supply side, more than 70 percent of oil and gas resources are controlled by states.

The Nexus Between Energy and Politics

Energy Politics discusses the relationship between energy and international politics. It focuses on the politics of oil and natural gas since, more than any other energy sources, their production, transport, and supply are entwined in international politics. It reaches a number of major findings.

• Energy and politics are inseparable. Energy trends and international politics are innately interconnected and energy security is an integral part of the foreign and national security policies of states.

• Energy use affects the structure of the international system itself: oil use creates an element of interdependency in the international system. Since oil is a global commodity, each country's demand affects the price and supply availability of oil for all consumers.

• Tight oil market conditions lead to increased internationalization of domestic political developments in oil producers and key transit states. Under tight conditions in the world oil markets, local political instability in an oil exporter or major transit state can have international reverberations.

• Energy creates an additional link between the domestic and foreign policies of states. The impact of hydrocarbon use on climate change, energy prices, and concerns about energy supply availability have made a state's domestic energy consumption habits and policies a matter of international political interest and concern.

• Oil-exporting states often adopt policies of resource nationalism in periods of tight oil market conditions. Such policies generally defy economic logic and thus tend to inhibit a state's oil production. In addressing energy security in the past, the real question was oil supplies.

• In the current era, natural gas is at the center of energy security policies due to its extreme vulnerability to political influence. In fact, the gas trade is much more vulnerable to political influence than the oil trade. With a rise in the global use of natural gas and surging cross-border natural gas trade, there is more opportunity for politics to affect energy supply relations.

• "Peace pipelines"—an oil or natural gas pipeline routed between countries in conflict as a means to achieve peace—are so far a chimera. There are no cases to date of successful so-called peace pipelines. Despite the frequent promotion of such proposals by U.S. and European policymakers, the establishment of energy export infrastructures has not contributed to conflict resolution in major disputes between states. Participating states and investors tend to require positive cooperative and stable relations prior to establishing major infrastructure energy supply projects between states. Otherwise, they would be loath to risk such a long-term commitment with only a long-term future payoff. Where energy infrastructure exists between countries that do not enjoy good relations, such as those in the former Soviet Union, it often becomes a source of tension or a symbolic battlefield.

• Oil exporters rarely stop the flow of supplies. Most effective oil embargos are conducted by consuming states (such as the U.S. embargo on Iran and the previous UN embargo on Iraq). Despite Venezuela's anti-U.S. rhetoric, the United States is still Caracas's main export market.

• When suppliers and consumers are interdependent in the supply relationship, the gas supply between them is generally stable and less vulnerable to political and security ebbs and tides. Whether the relations are dependent or interdependent seems to depend on a number of factors: symmetry in the extent of dependence of a supplier and a consumer (often connected to the size of the market in question) and the extent to which each side possesses alternative supply or market options, including transport infrastructure.

• Transit countries tend to use the energy weapon, while suppliers and consumers use it infrequently. This has been seen in Ukraine and Belarus, which have at times inhibited the flow of Russian oil and gas to markets in Western Europe in an attempt to attain political and economic goals.

• Multistate, lengthy, and expensive energy export projects that would have been dismissed out of hand in previous decades are almost commonplace today. This is a direct result of the trend of exporting oil also from challenging locations, such as landlocked states like Kazakhstan, Azerbaijan, and Chad.

• The connection between the drive to control oil and energy as a cause for interstate wars and its role in intrastate conflict is not proved. At the same time, the drive by most states to exploit additional energy sources is a potential source of border delimitation conflicts between states.

• The energy trade's physical security is vulnerable. This includes the main sea-lanes at the naval choke points of Strait of Hormuz, Strait of Malacca, and Bosporus Straits. Energy infrastructure has also become an attractive target for terrorist groups and a focus in civil strife.

• The major energy-consuming markets are privatizing and unbundling energy production, transport, and supply, while energy production is becoming more and more concentrated in the hands of states. This has created an uneven playing field between consumers and producers, which provides the opportunity for state-held producers like Russia's Gazprom to gain control of a significant chunk of infrastructure.

• In order to enhance energy security, states dependent on energy imports should expand their energy storage capacity. Doing so does not require cooperation with other states, yet is effective in averting crisis situations. Despite this, few states maintain sufficient energy storage capacity.

• Major energy exporters have distinctive patterns of economic and political development. Oil exporters are among the states with the highest foreign debt, lowest rate of democratic governance, and lowest levels of human development. Accordingly, few of the policy tools and prescriptions that are relevant for democracy promotion are applicable to major energy exporters.

• China, which has been designated a major energy consumer and potential competitor for energy supplies for the twenty-first century, shares with the United States a number of interests in the energy sphere.

While China's economic rise creates a number of adjustment challenges for regional and international security systems, access to energy supply need not be a major issue of contention, especially with the United States. The activity and investments of China's energy companies add volumes to world oil supplies, and China is successful in a number of locations around the globe where Western companies do not tend to thrive. In the future, competition for energy supplies actually is more likely between the European Union and China, over Russia's gas supplies. Once Moscow sells to both Europe and China, it will be in a position to play the two markets against each other for higher prices.

• The threat of climate change may serve as the catalyst for major long-term change in global dependence on fossil fuels. Climate change is no longer considered an issue relating to quality of life and environment, but one that directly affects human and global security.

The Era of Hydrocarbon Man

The age in which we live has been deemed the era of "hydrocarbon man." What we consume, how we live, the way we wage war, even the means of entertainment available to us have all been shaped by our access to energy produced by fossil fuels.

Beginning with the twentieth century, oil has been the strategic resource for the functioning of industrialized economies and the conduct of modern warfare. The starting point of oil as a strategic resource was the conversion of the British Royal Navy from coal to oil in 1912. This decision had a direct impact on British imperial policy: London subsequently became dependent on Iranian oil instead of domestically produced coal. During World War I, most of the participating armies also shifted to oil in large quantities. When World War I began, the British force in France had fewer than 1,000 motor vehicles. When the war ended, it had over 110,000 trucks, cars, and motorcycles—and several hundred tanks.[4] During World War II, access to oil was a key strategic goal of the warring powers, and was a major factor in the outcome of a number of campaigns.

During the first half of the twentieth century, oil production and supply were mainly controlled by seven U.S.- and European-based oil companies.[5] Nationalization of oil production only took place in the Soviet Union in 1917 and in Mexico in 1938. Moreover, until the 1970s the U.S. government and the governments in other large consuming countries regularly set oil prices. A little-noticed but important development took place during the 1960s, however. U.S. spare oil-production capacity shrank as consumption grew and investors underinvested in additional capacity amid low oil prices.

Another major shift in oil production took place in the 1970s, when most Middle East producers—and some other important producers such as Venezuela—nationalized their petroleum industries. Consequently, the bulk of the production market went from private ownership by international oil companies to state ownership by national oil companies. Today, over 75 percent of the world's proven oil reserves are in the hands of national oil companies. Also, 16 of the top 20 oil companies in the world are national oil companies. The top seven international oil companies—Exxon, BP, Royal Dutch Shell, Total, Chevron, Conoco-Phillips, and ENI—control less than 5 percent of the globe's reserves. This greatly influences investment and production trends and increases the interplay between politics and oil.

In 1960, five oil-producing countries—Iraq, Iran, Kuwait, Saudi Arabia, and Venezuela—formed the Organization of Petroleum Exporting Countries (OPEC) in an effort to offset the control of the major international oil companies in oil production and distribution. Today, OPEC's membership includes thirteen states. However, OPEC, with Saudi Arabia emerging as its leader, had its greatest impact in 1973–74, with the declaration of an oil embargo on the United States, Israel, and the Netherlands following the 1973 Yom Kippur War. The declared embargo did not lead to actual suspension of supplies to any states. But due to the already tight conditions of the world market on the eve of the declaration, the insecurity and uncertainty created by the war and the embargo declaration triggered a 400 percent increase in world oil prices in a short period. This price jump was sparked not by the boycott, however, but by the previous decline in spare U.S. oil production. These tight market conditions allowed OPEC's declaration to further boost already rising oil prices. In periods when oil production significantly outstretches demand, these political declarations and developments have less impact on oil prices. For example, previous declarations of boycotts by oil exporters, such as during the Suez crisis (1956) and the Six Day War (1967), had inconsequential effects on the market. However, this rapid price spike and an additional spike in 1979 following Iran's Islamic Revolution left policymakers around the globe with a lasting dread of depending on oil.

Throughout the 1970s and the early 1980s, OPEC was able to hold sway over international oil prices because of Saudi Arabia's significant spare oil production capacity. By using this spare capacity to lower and raise production, Saudi Arabia could control prices and subsequently affect political events. However, beginning in the mid-1980s, a major shift again took place in the dynamics of the world market with the coming on line of major production volumes from a number of non-OPEC sources, the breakdown in coordination among OPEC members, and the diminishing spare capacity of Saudi Arabia and other OPEC members.

The state of the world oil and energy markets in the early twenty-first century is fundamentally different from that of the 1970s. First and foremost, the relative production share of non-OPEC energy sources has continued to grow, and OPEC's grip on the market has been weakened significantly.[6] In 1982, non-OPEC production overtook OPEC production for the first time, a lead it has since maintained. Most non-OPEC producers have preferred to sell their oil on spot (that is, indirect) open markets. This trend has changed the nature of oil trade, since it is the dominant form of oil sales.

Moreover, the oil price peak of the mid-1970s as well as environmental concerns and technological developments led to changes in world consumption patterns. Conservation policies and technological advances that increased energy efficiency spurred a dramatic decrease in the share of oil use as part of global energy consumption in the early 1980s. In response to the oil crisis, the United States in 1975 enacted extensive legislation that mandated fuel efficiency for automobiles. Due to this and other measures, a little over a decade later the United States was 25 percent more fuel efficient and 32 percent more oil efficient than during the 1973 crisis.[7] In parallel, through extensive taxes on gasoline, the EU member states and Japan successfully slowed growth in oil consumption. While the absolute quantity of oil consumed globally has grown since the 1970s, its share of world energy consumption has declined. In contrast, the relative share of world use of nuclear energy, and especially natural gas, has grown significantly.[8] In the 1970s, oil shocks prompted the world's highly industrial states to move a number of energy functions from oil to natural gas and a portion of their electricity generation to nuclear energy.

Significantly, the structure of the U.S. economy has changed dramatically since the 1970s, with the United States consuming less than half the energy per dollar of gross national product (GNP) as it did in the 1970s. Energy-intensive manufacturing has declined in the United States, and the relationship between energy prices and economic growth has lessened. Sustained high oil prices no longer automatically entail immediate recession in the United States.

A sign of the shift in the dynamics of the world oil market can be found in the reaction of the market to the 2006 war in Lebanon between Israel and the Hezbollah militia. Previously, wars in the Middle East tended to lead to extended high oil prices. The initial days of the war caused a jump in prices, especially at the stage when it was not clear whether Iran would become directly involved, and whether the hostilities could lead to incidents that could affect traffic through the Strait of

Hormuz. However, after the initial impact of the war, oil prices stabilized, and the duration of the war did not have a major effect on world oil prices. In fact, an accident along the Druzhba pipeline from Russia to Eastern Europe in July 2006 had a greater impact on prices than the war. Thus, world oil prices appear to be no longer directly related to the state of the Arab-Israeli conflict.

Another new dimension of energy and international politics in the early twenty-first century is the emergence of energy oligarchs. These tycoons made their fortune through the acquisition of oil and gas riches, primarily in the teetering former Soviet Union. Armed with fortunes larges than the GNPs of some states, this group has influenced energy trends and politics—both domestically in a number of states and at times internationally.[9] These independent economic giants tend to promote global political agendas (and fund political and other activities directed at a number of states). They often reside in states other than their native lands or countries of citizenship, and possess multiple citizenships, creating global law enforcement complications for crimes such as money laundering that demand international cooperation. Many of the oligarchs buy into energy infrastructure around the globe, such as oil refineries and transportation infrastructure.

In 2005 and 2006, a major development emerged in the world system that may signal the end of the boundless reign of hydrocarbon man. Scientists from a variety of relevant disciplines began to unite behind an international consensus that the earth's climate is changing rapidly and that this development could lead to catastrophic effects for humanity. They also concluded that these climate changes were a consequence of human activity, especially carbon dioxide emissions from burning fossil fuels. This scientific consensus was coupled with a dramatic rise in incidents of catastrophic weather (intense typhoons and hurricanes, droughts and floods), in addition to other extraordinary weather (lack of snow in winter and intensely hot, long summers in Europe, record hot summers in the United States). Accordingly, public support has grown for adopting policies designed to avert catastrophic climate changes, and it is becoming politically costly for the United States and other countries to neglect doing so. Thus, states may adopt changes that will affect the uninhibited production of energy from fossil fuels. Climate change has even come to be discussed as a human security issue by the UN secretary general and Security Council.

Energy Sources

In analyzing the relationship between energy and politics, it is important to realize that the political dynamics of oil and gas are fundamentally different. The chief differences emerge from the fact that oil is a fungible commodity, while natural gas is not. Previous works on energy and politics have tended to focus on the politics connected to oil. In contrast, this book also discusses the role of natural gas supply in the politics between states. Natural gas supply is particularly vulnerable to political influences because of the direct and long-term nature of natural gas supply relations. The next section will present background information on the major sources of global energy: oil, natural gas, coal, and nuclear energy. Other noteworthy sources of global energy include hydropower, combustible renewables and waste, and small percentages of other renewables.

A Note on the Numbers

Statistics relating to the production, consumption, and reserves of primary energy sources are published regularly. Among the main sources are those provided by major industry players, such as BP and ENI. In addition, the U.S. government, through the Energy Information Agency of the U.S. Department of Energy, along with the U.S. Geological Survey of the U.S. Department of Interior, publishes energy data. The International Energy Agency publishes comprehensive data on energy production and consumption, as does OPEC. In addition, commercial sources provide a plethora of such data.

These different sources produce quite different data. Some of these discrepancies result from different research approaches, some from the fact that most of those that publish the data are major actors in energy policy and thus have vested interests in promoting or highlighting certain trends. In addition, most of the world's main oil exporters do not explain how they compute their volumes, which means that there is no certainty about the validity of their data. A question hangs over the status of even the oil volumes declared by Saudi Arabia, the world's most important oil exporter. OPEC member states have an inherent interest in distorting reports on their reserves, since their quotas within the cartel are set on the basis of reserves. When reading published data, one should take into consideration the source of the data and the biases it may reflect.

All the statistics concerning future volume and consumption trends should be treated as educated speculation. Two of the most important factors influencing energy production and consumption are technology and price. Since the future trends of both factors are unpredictable, no one can make precise estimates of future energy volumes and consumption trends. Moreover, high prices render certain geological and geopolitical locations and unconventional oil commercially attractive, which can lead to increased volumes. They also spur innovation to find new oil and change consumption habits through conservation and developing energy efficiency technology and new modes of transport and operation. Thus, at best the published data on future trends and volumes should be read with the assumption that no major technology developments will emerge in the period of the estimation that would significantly affect energy production or energy efficiency, and that prices remain within a typical range.

When comparing data on state energy consumption patterns, energy intensity, and climate-altering gas emissions, comparisons are generally made between states on the basis of population and by GNP. Clearly, these two indicators produce considerably different results. For example, in analyzing climate-altering emissions, developing countries like China and India, with their large populations, emphasize data based on population size. In contrast, the United States points to a relatively low emissions rate when analyzing emissions according to the size of its GNP.

Energy production data are divided into proven and estimated reserves. In states that are relatively veteran producers, the proven reserves are much larger than the estimated reserves, since in areas with vast exploration and extensive production, the geological picture is clearer. In newer producers, such as the states of the former Soviet Union, there is generally a large gap between the proven and the estimated reserves, since many fields are still unexplored. Thus, in analyzing data, one should not ignore the estimated reserve volumes, which in most cases will materialize into proven reserves as production advances.

Oil

Oil is the largest component of the world total primary energy supply (TPES), a one-third share. Oil is a popular energy source because it can be easily and cheaply transported and because it has flexible applications, including a range of uses: to generate electricity, provide heat and transportation, and fuel industry. Other fossil fuels can substitute for oil for most of these functions. However, current modes of transportation were developed based on the availability of copious and mostly inexpensive quantities of oil during the twentieth century. Widespread and inexpensive access to petroleum products meant that in the second part of the twentieth century there were few dramatic changes in the prevailing modes of transportation. For example, commercial flight time between London and New York has not changed significantly in 50 years. In the transportation sector, there are no good substitutes for oil, unless radical changes are made in the way people transport themselves and goods.

Oil is a global commodity with an integrated world price, established by average price at a given moment in a number of the main world trading centers. Two characteristics of oil affect a given barrel's price in relation to the world price: whether it is "sweet" or "sour" and whether it is "heavy" or "light." Sweet or sour refers to the percentage of sulfur in the oil. Since most final fuel products require that the sulfur be cleansed, the refining process for sour oil is more expensive and thus the raw fuel commands a lower price. Heavy or light refers to the density of the oil. The density of the oil is an indicator of the expected yield during the refining process: lighter oil provides a higher yield of petroleum products than heavy oil, and so therefore also affects the price. Oil density is expressed in degrees of API gravity, a standard of the American Petroleum Institute. Light oil, often called conventional oil, is the most common type of oil produced globally. During periods of high oil prices, commercial interest often grows in developing heavy and extra-heavy oil. Venezuela's large reservoir of untapped oil in the Orinoco Belt is heavy oil. Canada possesses extensive volumes of tar sands that could produce huge volumes of extra-heavy oil.

As stated above, it is difficult to estimate precisely future volumes and consumption trends because of the inability to forecast two major determinants: technological advances and price. Such caveats should also be kept in mind in assessing claims related to "peak oil"—that is, the anticipated end of oil. While oil is presumed to be a finite commodity, and the insights of the geologists who have published their assessments of different production locations are instructive, a definitive answer on the future volumes of oil in the world cannot be given if we cannot anticipate future technological advances. Indeed, it is common during periods of high oil prices for publications to appear forecasting the end of oil, only to be found on the remainder shelf when prices fall again.

The oil industry is divided into two major sectors: upstream and downstream. Upstream activity refers to oil exploration and production. Downstream activity refers to oil refining, petrochemical plants, transport, and distribution. After crude oil is extracted from the ground, it is processed in oil refineries, which produce the various products such as gasoline, industrial fuels, jet fuel, and home and heating fuel.

The cost of oil production varies from location to location. Technologically complex extraction can drive up production costs. Landlocked sources such as Chad and the Caspian basin also must pay more for pipeline transit prior to reaching a port. The Persian Gulf producers have some of the lowest oil production costs.

Today's largest oil producers are Saudi Arabia, Russia, and the United

States. The largest exporters are Saudi Arabia, Russia, and Iran, with the United States the world's largest oil importer.

Natural Gas

Natural gas is the world's fastest growing primary energy source. Global consumption is anticipated to double by 2030. Natural gas will soon overtake coal as the second most important energy source, and among the Organization for Economic Cooperation and Development (OECD) countries it has already supplanted it. If current trends continue, natural gas consumption will overtake that of oil within a couple of decades and become the leading global energy source. Natural gas is especially attractive because it releases significantly lower emissions that cause air pollution and lead to climate change.

The drawback of natural gas is that under current technologies it is not as easily transportable as oil or coal. Natural gas is moved predominantly by pipeline, with a little over 5 percent by liquefied natural gas (LNG) tankers. However, imported gas commands only a third of the world's consumption of natural gas. Its transport infrastructures require long-term investments that see payback only if contracts remain in place for as long as 15 to 20 years.

In contrast to the oil trade, a direct connection exists between producers and consumers of natural gas. Natural gas prices are set in individually agreed-upon contracts. In some deals, the sides agree to link the price of the supplied gas to changes in world oil prices, while others establish a price that is independent of oil prices. When establishing new natural gas pipelines, many contracts are concluded on a "take or pay" basis that obligates the customer to commit to purchase a set amount of natural gas, regardless of whether or not it is actually consumed.

There is a growing trade in liquefied natural gas. LNG is traded mostly in the form of bilateral contracts, but LNG spot markets are emerging. As the trade expands, it will most likely evolve toward a global market. The world's largest LNG exporter is Qatar, with a third of such exports. The three main importers are Japan, South Korea, and Taiwan, which import 70 percent of the world's LNG. Asian imports are expected to expand since China and India are building regasification facilities.

Coal

Coal accounts for a quarter of the world's energy supply. Coal is the predominant source of electricity production in the world. In a number of Asian countries, it is the primary source of total energy consumed; in China it comprises two-thirds of the primary energy supply. The majority of the world's recoverable coal reserves are found in four countries: the United States (27 percent), Russia (17 percent), China (13 percent), and India (10 percent). Coal is in wide use due to its relatively low cost, especially in electricity production, and the extensive reserves of exporters that make it low risk in terms of security of supply. Today, coal accounts for 50 percent of electricity production in the United States.

Coal's major drawback is the pollutants it emits. Coal-burning plants are the major source of climate-altering greenhouse gases, and, depending on the type of plant, a source of significant air pollutants. To be sure, state-of-the-art supercritical pulverized coal (PC) generation coal-fired electricity plants produce significantly lower air pollution emissions than previous generations. But significant research and investment efforts are needed in carbon dioxide capture and sequestration (CCS) if coal is going to continue in widespread use without its baleful impact on climate change.[10]

There has long been an interest in liquid coal as a substitute for oil. Technologies are in use to produce high-quality diesel fuel, naphtha, and LPG from coal. Coal to liquids is attractive as a means to enhance security of energy supply, but still must contend with its impact on climate change.

Nuclear Energy

Nuclear energy primarily is used to produce electricity. Following the 1970s oil crisis, the nuclear energy industry experienced significant growth, but still provides less than 7 percent of the world's energy consumption and 17 percent of the world's electricity production. The largest impediment to nuclear energy is its cost: it is significantly more expensive to produce electricity from nuclear energy than from fossil fuels. Still, due to the rising threat of climate change, nuclear energy is becoming increasingly attractive since the nuclear reactors themselves do not omit greenhouse gases when operating and the entire process of producing nuclear energy generates limited amounts of climate altering gases and air pollutants. On the flip side, handling and storage of nuclear waste created by the nuclear energy industry creates long-term environmental and security concerns, as do potential accidents at nuclear reactors. In addition, expanding the use of nuclear energy increases the material and technology and the number of engineers and scientists available for employment in nuclear weapons programs, and thus increases the threat of nuclear proliferation. Moreover, global uranium supplies are limited and located in a small number of states, creating concerns for long-term supply reliability.

The world's largest producers of nuclear energy are the United States,

France, Japan, Germany, and Russia. In percentage of domestic electricity produced by nuclear energy, the leading states are France, Sweden, and Ukraine. In France, nearly 80 percent of electricity is generated by nuclear energy. Following the 1970s oil crisis, the French government made nuclear energy a national project and nurtured the industry's development.

Oil Prices

Oil is the most traded commodity in the world; thus, it is one of the crucial inputs to the world economy. Oil prices are determined globally, and its trade occurs on world markets. Oil is a fungible commodity: producer and consumer need not be directly linked, and a change in supply and demand anywhere affects prices everywhere. Thus, the dynamics of the global energy market increase interdependency between states in the international system.

Oil prices have a cyclical nature: low oil prices lead to high demand, accompanied by low investment in oil production and refining and low interest in conservation and use of other fuels (such as natural gas, nuclear energy, and renewable energy sources). Consequently, as supplies constrict, prices rise (the "market tightens"), which in the long term leads to a reduction of demand (often encouraged through government policies such as conservation and higher energy consumption taxes). Tight market conditions lead to increased investment in production, with consequently increased supply. Other fuels become economically competitive, and in the long run economic recession often emerges—both of which lessen the demand for oil. Thus, a rise in oil prices is followed by a decline, which may manifest as a price crash: earlier investments in production lead to additional supplies becoming available at the time demand is dwindling.

These oil price cycles are large, spanning a number of years—usually decades. Policies of producers and consumers affect the length of the segments of the cycles. Additional factors also affect long-term oil consumption trends: the price cycle is influenced by factors that are not directly connected to oil prices, such as demography (population increases or declines), changes in GNP, and urbanization trends. These factors had a large impact on the energy demand that increased on the eve of the twenty-first century with a subsequent surge in world oil prices.

Within these swings there are, from time to time, price shocks and crashes that upset the cyclic nature of the trend. These sharp shocks can be caused by political shocks such as the two Gulf wars. Downward crashes can be caused by the coming online of new sources or massive disease outbreaks or security threats (such as September 11) that discourage people from travel. In 1986, world oil prices experienced a major crash from which they took almost two decades to fully recover. While most oil importers have the price spikes of 1973 and 1979 imprinted on their memory, the major Gulf producers have the 1986 price crash influencing their policy priorities.

One of the reasons oil prices move in such cycles is that when oil prices are low there is no incentive for new production, especially in areas where oil is relatively expensive to extract, and little incentive for investments in oil infrastructure such as tankers, refineries, and rigs. When prices rise, it takes years of high prices to build these infrastructures, so they are generally in chronic shortage. In the energy market of the beginning of the twenty-first century, a major shortage of world oil refinery capacity exists.

Even in periods of high oil prices, investors are cautious in initiating production of new supplies and constructing infrastructure, since they are well aware of the pattern of prices and that they will likely go down. Companies and oil-producing states generally operate on the basis of conservative estimates for oil prices in judging whether proposed projects are worthy.

Toward the end of the twentieth century, oil prices entered the high price stage of the cycle. In the 1990s, encouraged by low oil prices and economic growth, world demand for oil increased dramatically. This rising demand was primarily driven by increased U.S. consumption (concurrent with a decline of 2 million barrels a day in domestic production), and sustained rise in Asian consumption. These prices remained high because of population growth and urbanization in Asia and rising GNP in the United States and Asia. This high price period was especially long, since both the U.S. and European economies have proven to be resilient to high oil prices.

The decade of resilience of the Western economies is a result of greatly increased energy efficiency, which was spurred by the soaring oil prices of the 1970s. As noted, many economic sectors have also moved from oil to other fuels, such as natural gas. At the beginning of the twenty-first century, the United States uses half the oil it did in the 1970s to produce the same GNP.

The 1970s surge in oil prices led to the establishment of the International Energy Agency (IEA) in 1974 as a tool to create energy security, initially for North Atlantic Treaty Organization (NATO) countries in the larger framework of the OECD states, whose mission was to build and coordinate stocks of oil to prevent future shortages. In addition, the United States created the Strategic Petroleum Reserve (SPR). This, along with IEA stocks, has created a dramatic change in the oil price mechanisms. The building of stocks by the IEA, states, and corporations has put in place buffers in the world oil market, which can lessen the blows of tight oil market conditions.

Governments could, of course, do more to curb high prices: the governments of both the leading and rising consumers have not enacted serious policy measures that could curb oil use, such as higher energy consumption taxes. Some governments, especially in Asia and in energy-exporting states, continue to subsidize energy consumption. Government fuel subsidies have been a major factor contributing to extensive energy consumption.

Oil prices are also affected by a factor that is independent of consumption and production trends: the trading of oil stocks. In 1983, the flotation of oil on the New York Mercantile Exchange was initiated and spread to exchanges around the globe, and is a significant vector of economic activity.

Not Hydrocarbon Man for All

The sources of energy in use and access to electricity create variations in lifestyles around the globe. While "hydrocarbon man" prevails in industrialized societies and urban centers, one-quarter of the world population—some 1.6 billion people—have no access to electricity.[11] Half the world's households use solid fuels (biomass and coal) for cooking and heating at home in devices that produce significant indoor pollution. Most of these households are in India, China, and sub-Saharan Africa. Home energy use of coal and biomass causes significant health damages that are estimated to be responsible for 4 to 5 percent of the world's illness costs. Women and children are most exposed to the pollutants produced by indoor stoves since they tend to spend more time at home, and thus they incur higher rates of related illness. In China, coal is in widespread use in home stoves, exposing millions of people to indoor pollutants. According to the UNDP World Energy Assessment, the total amount of health-damaging pollution released from home stoves worldwide is not high relative to that from fossil fuels, but because human exposure to the indoor pollutants is much higher than to the outdoor pollution created by fossil fuels, the health effects are higher.[12] In addition, solid biomass fuels have high rates of climate-altering emissions.

The variation in access to energy sources creates political challenges. Assistance in helping homes move up the "energy ladder" to less health-damaging fuels for home use is part of the agenda of a number of governments and international aid programs. However, this will require massive funds, often at the expense of other urgent needs such as clean water and education. Energy "haves" and "have nots" may become a prominent issue on the international development agenda.

Energy in International Relations and Political Science

Despite the centrality of energy to a state's national security, the effects energy has on domestic politics and regime development, and the role of energy in international relations, the professional journals in international relations and political science have paid scant attention to publishing research on the topic. For example, *International Security*, the flagship journal in international relations and security studies, has in its thirty-year history published only eight articles devoted to energy.[13] A 1995 special issue that maps new, nonmilitary threats in the international system has not one article devoted to energy.[14] In contrast, topics such as water and environment do appear in the volume. Policy-oriented journals such as *Foreign Affairs* and *Foreign Policy* have published extensively on topics related to energy, however, and a number of noteworthy academic books have been published on energy and politics.[15]

During periods of tight energy market conditions, there has generally been an increase in scholarly publications dealing with energy. For instance, following the 1973–74 oil crisis, a number of publications in major political science and international relations outlets appeared that dealt with energy. Among the most noteworthy is *Energy and Security*, edited by Joseph Nye with David Deese, based on a major research project conducted at Harvard University.[16]

Topics that have been examined in major journals and books on the field of energy and politics include OPEC's use of the "oil weapon,"[17] the impact of civilian nuclear energy production on the proliferation of nuclear weapons,[18] the role in international politics of major multinational energy corporations,[19] the impact of oil imports on arms sales to oil exporters,[20] state strength and oil shocks,[21] and the IEA.[22] Political science works have devoted extensive research to the impact of oil (and other mineral) exports on economic and regime development.[23] In addition, the role of oil in interstate and intrastate conflicts has been researched extensively in recent years.[24]

This volume will build on this previous work and also go further in its analysis. It will provide a comprehensive look at the interaction between energy and politics in the international system, focusing on the dynamics of oil and natural gas.

Chapter 1
Energy and Regime Type

Major energy exporters possess distinctive patterns of economic and political development. Revenues from oil and gas exports affect the economies of exporting states in a different way than revenue derived from exports of manufactured and other produced goods and services. Almost counterintuitively, oil exporters tend to fare more poorly economically than energy-poor states. Furthermore, because of the volatile nature of oil prices, the economies of major oil producers are generally unstable. Moreover, nondemocratic states that derive the majority of their income from energy exports are considerably less likely to make a transition to democracy. A major foreign policy implication of this development is that U.S.-led democratization policies are most likely inapplicable to major oil producers.

In analyzing the impact of energy production on economic and regime development, a number of variables must be differentiated. First, a distinction should be made between energy producers and energy exporters. Income derived from energy sales abroad has a distinctive effect on states. Second, it is necessary to distinguish between energy reserves owned mainly by private sources versus those owned by the state. Third, one should differentiate between energy exporters and major energy exporters: the International Monetary Fund (IMF) draws a distinction between major energy exporters, in which (among other criteria) over 40 percent of the gross domestic product (GDP) is derived from energy export revenues and other energy exporters.[1] The economic and political trends discussed for energy producers are most applicable to major energy exporters.

Economies of Resource Exporters

Energy-poor states often look at their energy-rich counterparts with envy, and strive to find local energy sources. Economists Jeffrey Sachs and Andrew Warner, however, conducted an extensive empirical analysis of

97 countries over 1971–1989 that shows that economies with abundant
natural resources have tended to grow less rapidly than economies with
scarce natural resources.[2] This has often been dubbed the "resource
curse." Stanford University's Terry Lynn Karl has labeled it "the paradox
of plenty."[3] She claims that oil exporting is the most important factor
influencing development in states of this type. Despite vast cultural, geo-
graphical, and geostrategic conditions, major oil-exporting states display
similar paths of economic and political development.[4]

Energy export revenues also impair the growth of nonenergy sectors
and thus the sustainability of the economies of energy exporters. The
economies of major energy exporters tend to display a shift in labor and
capital away from the agricultural sectors, and in many cases, from the
manufacturing sectors as well. For example, higher wages in the energy
export sector, often provided by foreign companies, attract labor from
other sectors. The economic boom associated with oil and gas exports
also often raises the value of the local currency, rendering locally produced products expensive, increasing imports, and decreasing exports
of goods produced by the nonoil sectors. This phenomenon is referred
to as "Dutch Disease."[5] Few states that have been heavily dependent on
the oil sector have succeeded in simultaneous development of the nonoil sector, and this affects their long-term stability.[6] Norway and Indonesia are notable exceptions.

The cyclical nature of energy, and especially oil profits, places the
energy export state in a cycle of boom and bust that has important implications for state stability. During times of high energy prices and thus
large state revenues, energy exporters tend to undertake large-scale state
spending, often aimed at satisfying popular demands. When prices inevi-
tably fall, oil-producing states are left with large public expectations
without the ability to meet public demands, which in turns leads to fiscal
crises. In contrast to most predictions following the oil boom of the
1970s, OPEC oil exporters found themselves on the eve of the twenty-
first century not only with the real price of crude oil lower than the 1973
level, but also with extensive debt and significant economic challenges.[7]

The revenue produced by energy exports has a different effect on the
producer's economy than that created by manufactured and services
exports. Energy-export-derived revenue produces scant employment
and does not generate significant linkages with other economic sectors.
Except for service sectors, it does not generally spur significant additional economic activity.

In addition, oil export states have poor capacity for economic reform.
Energy exporters do not tend to undertake reform of underdeveloped
economic sectors during the boom periods, and they rarely have the
capacity to do so during the dry periods. Moreover, during prosperous

times, energy exporters often use energy profits to subsidize underdeveloped sectors, but these subsidies are hard to maintain during periods of low energy-export income. Delayed or avoided economic reforms and stringency measures damage the oil exporters' long-term economic composure.

In reality, few major oil exporters have full market economies. Energy export profits empower the state and endow it with an economic allocation function. Thus, market forces cannot govern the economy. The limited private sector is also dependent on state contracts and permission of the state to conduct its affairs. The swollen bureaucracies supported by the state also serve as an obstacle to economic liberalization and a production-oriented economy.[8]

An additional factor that weighs down the economies of oil-exporting countries is their tendency to maintain low domestic energy costs through extensive price subsidies. Venezuela, for example, spent $9 billion in 2006 to keep gasoline prices significantly below world levels. Iran spends on average $20 billion annually, 15 percent of its economic output, to maintain low domestic energy costs and other subsidies. These subsidies create conditions for the extensive smuggling of gasoline and other products to bordering states and chronic energy shortages in Iran. Moreover, subsidized energy leads to inefficiency in its use.

To be sure, some oil exporters are taking steps not to repeat past mistakes by restraining spending increases during boom periods, increasing investments abroad, reducing oil production to lengthen the oil boom, and banking oil revenues in long-term funds. In terms of spending restraint, recently some oil exporters with small populations and large oil exports, have displayed relatively prudent behavior in limiting the expansion of the public sector. By contrast, states with large populations—particularly those with modest oil exports—have not resisted the temptation to use the newly acquired oil revenues to expand state spending.[9]

During the 1970s oil boom, most of the major producers allocated an unprecedented amount of their revenue—between a quarter and a half—to domestic investment.[10] Their economies were not suited to absorb such large investments and their investment decisions were often guided by noneconomic considerations or faulty investment assessments. By contrast, during the current windfall period, the major oil exporters with small populations are investing substantial amounts of their revenues abroad. For example, Caspian region energy exporters Kazakhstan and Azerbaijan are investing substantial funds in the port states from which their oil is exported, Turkey and Georgia.

Major OPEC producers also refrained from expanding production, having attempted to lengthen the period of high oil prices. This behavior contradicts earlier periods, when OPEC preferred to maintain moderate prices to prevent major oil-consuming countries from enacting conservation measures or increasing use of fuels other than oil. OPEC's new measures to sustain high oil prices may in the short run have helped maintain the fiscal health of the oil exporters. However, in the long run this policy sets the stage for another major price and consumption crash, as it drives consumers to reduce their long-term consumption of oil.

In addition, following Norway's example, some energy exporters have established oil revenue funds to preserve investment monies for development of the nonoil sector and to save the revenues for future generations. Legislation allocates a set portion of the revenues derived from state-owned energy exports to be diverted to the state oil fund; these revenues are thus not designated for use in the state budget during oil booms. Some studies indicate that these funds can reduce spending trends and also reduce real exchange rate appreciation during periods of rising oil prices.[11] International financial organizations, such as the IMF, regularly encourage exporters to establish such funds and develop oversight mechanisms. The newly rising producers in the former Soviet Union, such as Kazakhstan and Azerbaijan, have made establishment of state oil funds a cornerstone of their policies in an attempt to elude the resource curse.

Each state, however, regulates its oil fund in line with its own national laws. In a number of nondemocratic states, the effectiveness of the legal regimes governing the use of the funds has come into question, and the political opposition often views these revenues as potential slush funds for the ruling government. At the same time, in some states, such as Azerbaijan, the state oil fund is one of the most transparently operated public entities.

Despite the poor economic showing of many major energy exporters and the increasing poverty in a number of them, international institutions such as the World Bank continue to promote resource extractive industries, such as oil, as a strategy for economic development. The World Bank maintains that under certain conditions the profits from oil exports can contribute to poverty reduction in countries that have few other viable economic opportunities. But it seems that in many cases wishful thinking prevails in policy attempts to circumvent the resource curse. There are no cases in which such prescriptions have succeeded, yet international institutions and academics continue to promote new plans.[12]

The most prominent case of World Bank promotion of oil exports, despite their downsides, is the Chad-Cameroon pipeline project, which became operational in 2003.[13] The project received extensive support from the World Bank, including funding participation and recruitment, and active participation in the oversight of the revenues derived. The goal in promoting the project was to contribute to poverty eradication in Chad through oil exports. As of late 2008, this experiment has not resulted in the declared goals. But after the oil revenues began to flow substantially, the Chad government abrogated the agreed-upon framework with the World Bank, which consequently canceled loans to Chad and that country's participation in other development programs.

The Political Regimes of Energy Exporters

Political scientists debate the factors that lead to the emergence of democracy; these include political culture, size and strength of the middle class, democratic tradition, strength of civil society, and war. Major oil exporters display a strong common tendency to be governed by nondemocratic regimes. Indeed, being a major energy exporter seems to be an overwhelming determinant factor in regime development. Few major oil exporters have transitioned to democracy if they were not democratic before major oil exports began. Moreover, a disproportionate number of nondemocratic states are significant energy producers. The wave of democratic transition that swept over many countries between the 1970s and 1990s affected all areas of the world—except the Middle East.[14] Generally, states with high GNPs moved to democracy; the Middle East's wealthy oil-exporting states did not make this jump. Apparently, wealth from energy exports (and other minerals) has a different impact on the development of political regimes than wealth derived from other sources.

In an attempt to explain the democracy deficit among energy producers, many political scientists view research on rentier economies as an important guide. In a rentier economy, three factors are present. First, income from natural resources is the most significant input into the economy. Second, the majority of this revenue is from abroad. Third, a small part of the population is engaged in generating these revenues, or rents.[15] A corollary to this last fact is that the state is the primary recipient of the rent revenue.[16]

The rentier state, instead of extracting revenue from the population through taxation, and thus having to earn legitimacy from the public, acts as a distributor of the earnings from exports. Giacomo Luciani refers to a state with a rentier economy as an "allocation state."[17] This distributor function strengthens the power of the state. Through an extensive welfare system, the rentier state purchases legitimacy. Energy export states tend to make large expenditures on public welfare, such as education, health, employment, and infrastructure. At the same time, the state denies the public the opportunity to constrain its behavior or change the ruling elite. Instead of "no taxation without representation," the rentier state is no taxation *and* no representation.

The oil-exporting states of the Middle East form the majority of the states that fit the rentier model. In her important essay, "Rentier State and Shi'a Islam in the Iranian Revolution," Theda Skocpol describes Iran under shah Mohammad Pahlavi on the eve of the Islamic Revolution:

> Under the second Shah, the domestic underpinnings of the Iranian state also changed as the state became increasingly addicted to revenues from exports of oil and natural gas. Iran's government became a "rentier state," awash in petro-dollars, and closely linked to the rhythms of the world capitalist economy. Especially after the mid-1960s, this state did not need to wrest taxes from its own people, and the economic basis of its revenues was an industry oriented primarily to exports, and employing only a tiny percentage of the labor force. The state's main relationships to Iranian society were mediated through its expenditures—on the military, on development projects, on modern construction, on consumption subsidies, and the like. Suspended above its own people, the Iranian state bought them off, rearranged their lives and repressed any dissidents among them.[18]

The rentier state also has discretionary power over how the revenue is spent, which means it can both co-opt and suppress political opposition. Major energy exporters with large populations tend to support large public-sector employment, in order to co-opt sizable segments of the population and create a positive attitude among the educated class toward the continued existence of the ruling regime. Accordingly, the 2007 budget proposed by Iranian president Mahmoud Ahmadinejad was nearly 25 percent larger than the 2005 budget; expenditures included a 31 percent increase for state enterprises.[19]

In many regimes, public economic demands are an important impetus to mobilizing the people for regime change. In contrast, in major energy exporters, the economic motive is absent. Those who are loyal to the regime receive economic benefits. Those who oppose it lose access to employment and benefits. Major oil exporter states tend to offer employment to university graduates, creating a large bureaucratic class beholden to the regime. Since the state is the largest employer, political opponents are generally deprived of good economic opportunities. Moreover, the dominance of the state in the economy prevents the emergence of an independent bourgeoisie or middle class, often the bastion of democratic transition. Furthermore, since the oil industry employs only a small number of people, and many of these are expatriates or can be replaced by oil companies through import of professional labor from abroad, powerful and independent trade unions do not tend to develop. This deprives major oil-exporting states of an additional potential flag bearer of democratic transition.

In a noteworthy essay on the link between energy export and democracy deficits, Michael Ross claims that the lack of democracy in oil-exporting states is explained by a combination of three factors: the "rentier effect," in which oil-rich governments use low tax rates and patronage to undercut demands for democratization and by which oil wealth is used to develop patronage; a "repression effect," in which oil revenues enable governments to boost their funding for internal security; and a "modernization effect," in which growth based on export of oil and minerals fails to bring about the social and cultural changes that tend to produce democratic government.[20]

Non-energy exporters with economies strongly affected by oil production in neighboring or foreign states often reveal attributes similar to the rentier states, and can be considered semi-rentiers or second-tier rentier states. Examples are Jordan, Egypt, and Georgia. These kinds of states derive significant income from energy-related sources such as operation of energy transit infrastructure in their territories and remittances of workers in energy-exporting countries.[21]

The Stability of Major Energy Exporters

Despite the boom-and-bust cycles of their economies and their dependence on revenue from energy sales abroad to run government operations, major energy-export regimes do not seem to be inherently less stable than other authoritarian regimes. Few regime changeovers have taken place in the major oil exporters since the 1970s.[22] In fact, energy revenue to the state may contribute to the longevity of the regime and allow inefficient regimes to stay in power, creating uniquely powerful but ineffective states. Even when a transition occurs, in the end most of these states have remained authoritarian regimes and oil-export-dependent rentier states. As Skocpol has shown, the Islamic Republic of Iran, like its predecessor, has been able to survive on oil profits, despite little ability to generate economic livelihood in Iran:

An Iranian Islamic Republic could remain, for quite some time, another sort of rentier state: a populist, welfare-oriented rentier state, with the ulama passing out alms in return for moral conformity on a grander scale than ever before. Unemployment and underemployment could continue at high levels in a stagnant national economy.[23]

It seems that when future transitions do take place, they will most likely be revolutionary (and most likely accompanied with violence), since it is unlikely that the large class of people whose livelihood and power is contingent on the existence of the ruling regimes will bow out easily. Moreover, while few major energy exporters have experienced regime transition since the amassment of their power in the 1970s, they have frequently been plagued by violence and public rioting at times when the regime was unable to deliver the expected goods, especially when oil prices were low.

The Democracy Deficit and the Energy Exporters of the Former Soviet Union

The fall of the Soviet Union created a number of new energy exporters: Kazakhstan, Azerbaijan, and Turkmenistan. These countries, alongside Russia, have a set of characteristics that make them nontypical major energy exporters. Accordingly, the type of political regime that may develop in these states may be different from that in the archetypical Middle Eastern energy exporter. Thus these states may succeed in transitioning to democracy, despite being major oil exporters.

Like the Middle East states, none of the former Soviet producers had become democracies before they began full-scale export of oil. Moreover, with the exception of Russia, most of the energy resources in these exporters are, like those in the Middle East, owned by state oil companies. However, unlike the Middle East producers, all the states of the former Soviet Union achieved full modernization prior to the Soviet breakup and the advent of independent oil export. These states and most of their populations are fully secularized. Besides having almost universal literacy, both men and women are highly educated, with women fully integrated into the work force. Social mobility and strong professional and commercial bonds between citizens traverse local identity. Moreover, the economies of the states were diverse and not dependent on energy exports before they became major energy exporters. In addition, the major energy exporters of the former Soviet Union conducted extensive economic reform and relatively liberalized their economies prior to the arrival of the bulk of oil export revenues.

The energy exports of these states have been developed in most cases in the framework of production sharing agreement (PSA) ownership partnerships with foreign energy companies. In recent decades, the international energy companies have generally been interested in transparency and preservation of rule of law in their partner states as a way to protect their vast investments. A number of the former Soviet states have accepted competitive market principles in energy resource production, in contrast to the producers in the Middle East. Accordingly, most of the post-Soviet oil exporters have active private markets in operation, again in contrast to their Middle East counterparts. In addition, the post-Soviet oil exporters have varied, active, and critical media outlets. These factors have the potential to allow these states to circumvent the democracy deficit of the other major energy exporters.

Policy Implications

Following the collapse of the Soviet Union, both the Clinton and Bush administrations made the spread of democracy a major U.S. policy goal. The two administrations set out to promote this goal with no tested or clear policy prescriptions. Thus, the United States has been actively involved in democracy promotion in the states that emerged in the former Soviet Union, while among the oil producers of the Middle East, with the exception of post-Saddam Iraq, the United States has treaded gingerly in democracy promotion. Moreover, the United States has often confused liberalization measures by the Middle East major oil producers with steps toward democracy.

There is no evidence that liberalization measures, such as allowing women to appear more in the public sphere and permitting some independent media outlets to operate, actually lead to democracy. In fact, it may be that these forms of liberalization, by releasing pent-up pressures, actually help regimes retain their grip. This seems likely in Iran, where the liberalization measures enacted under president Mohammad Khatami pulled the plug on the mounting reform movement by easing the life of citizens. Democracy is different from liberalization of the public space. It is about the ability of the populace to change the government at regular intervals. Nothing like this has occurred among the Middle East major oil producers, despite the fact that some have enacted some liberalization measures in recent years.

As the analysis in this chapter indicates, few of the tools and policy prescriptions that are relevant for the promotion of democracy in most states are applicable to major energy exporters. The power of the state and its grip on the economy, the inability of any other economic class to confront the state, and the lack of overlap between economic and political demands for most of the populace leave few effective measures that can be used to confront state power. It may be that these regimes are in reality nonreformable, and that most of their successors will operate in a similar manner, unless comprehensive reform takes place in their economies and the state is not the main recipient of energy export wealth. Only an alternative force backed up with strong economic means can challenge the monopoly of the state in most major energy exporters.

Chapter 2
Foreign Policy

Energy is both a factor that influences a state's foreign policy outcomes and a potential tool of foreign policy. Enhancing energy supply security is part of the national security agenda of energy-importing states, while the goal of assuring stable markets is on the policy agenda of exporting states. Stable access to oil, including during war time, is a component of military planning and national security policies, and lack of access creates a diminished military capacity. During periods of tight international energy market conditions, energy tends to become a more prominent factor and tool in states' foreign policies and a higher priority on their policy agenda. At these times, energy needs affect the foreign policies of importers as well as exporters.

One of the major developments of the early twenty-first century is the dramatic expansion of physical ties between states through energy infrastructure, mainly because of the increasing use of natural gas. This development fosters long-term linkages and at times dependencies between suppliers and consumers, and thus more room for politics. Stable political relations between producers and consumers are also a prerequisite in most cases to long-term pipeline linkages. Moreover, assessments of long-term political stability in concerned countries and in the relations between suppliers and consumers is an important consideration when investors assess a proposed infrastructure project.

The state of the world energy market affects broader international relations and vice versa. Oil use affects the structure of the international system itself: it creates an element of interdependency in the international system. Since oil is a global commodity, each country's demand affects the price and supply availability of oil for all consumers. In addition, instability and conflict in any major oil producer often affects oil prices worldwide.

Energy creates an additional link between a state's domestic and foreign policies. The impact of hydrocarbon use on climate change, rising energy prices, and concerns about energy supply availability have transformed domestic energy consumption habits and policies into a matter of international political interest. This internationalization can also be a source of conflict as states attempt to coerce others to change domestic energy taxation policies, adopt energy and fuel efficiency standards, and join international regimes that entail limitation of hydrocarbon use.

Politics is also playing an increasingly important role on the supply side with greater state involvement in the energy arena. More than 75 percent of the proven oil and gas reserves in the world are in the hands of national oil and gas companies. The state, directly or through the national companies, is often a major investor in production and export projects. Moreover, the state is often the regulator of these same projects and uses that function to promote its commercial and political interests. Russia, for example, has pointed to environmental considerations to justify pushing out foreign competitors in favor of Gazprom and Russian oil companies.

Energy supplies are frequently viewed by suppliers, consumers, and transit states as a potential tool to promote foreign policy and security goals. With rising European dependence on natural gas supplies from Russia, and a string of energy disputes between Russia and many of its former Soviet neighbors in 2005–2006, there has been considerable commentary warning about the danger of the "oil weapon" and the "gas weapon." For example, U.S. senator Richard Lugar (R-Ind.), a leading U.S. lawmaker on foreign policy issues, has stated that "the use of energy as an overt weapon is not a theoretical threat of the future; it is happening now."[1] Energy importers have attempted to formulate policies to reduce their vulnerability to these perceived threats. Yet, despite the rhetoric of policymakers and pundits in both supply and consumer states, intended major oil and gas supply disruptions have been few, and in most cases initiated not by suppliers or consumers, but by transit states.

A number of issues about the relationship between states' energy and foreign policies need to be examined. They include increased international interest in regime stability in key energy producers and transit states; resource nationalism; windfall profits and foreign policies of energy exporters; energy weapons and embargos; and relations between gas importers and exporters.

The New Focus on Political Developments in Energy Exporters

Tight oil market conditions lead to increased internationalization of domestic political developments in oil producers and key transit states. Domestic political turmoil in an oil-producing country—or its involvement in an armed conflict—can cause significant shocks in the world oil market. Examples include the impact of strikes in Venezuela (2003) and riots in Nigeria (2005) on global oil prices. Violent regime change and other revolutionary situations in oil-producing states generally lead to a shutdown of oil production, with producers often taking years to rebound. In the 1970s, the global trend of high oil prices was dramatically accelerated by the overthrow of the monarchy in Iran and the shutdown of the oil industry during the 1979 Revolution. Consequently, large energy importers take an assertive role in the domestic politics in energy-producing states.

In turn, energy interests, especially under tight international market conditions, affect the mapping of geostrategic interests. Because they are now oil exporters, countries such as Sudan, Chad, and Myanmar—which barely registered on the world geostrategic map two decades ago—have garnered international attention. In addition, energy transit states such as Turkey, Georgia, and Malaysia have augmented their geostrategic value. Domestic developments in Saudi Arabia, Russia, Iraq, Kazakhstan, Azerbaijan, Indonesia, Nigeria, and Venezuela continue to be of international interest. When oil prices are high, major world powers may be tempted to intervene more often in situations of unrest or in conflicts in energy-producing countries.

Even in less dramatic circumstances, oil importers have become increasingly involved in the domestic politics of oil producers. For instance, many foreign governments opposed Moscow's criminal proceedings against Mikhail Khodorkovsky, founder of the Russian oil company Yukos, and the subsequent dismantling of Yukos. Russian courts found Khodorkovsky guilty of fraud and tax evasion and sentenced him to a long prison term in Siberia. Many observers of the proceedings believe Khodorkovsky did not receive due process and was persecuted by the Russian government. Foreign policy interest in the criminal proceedings against Khodorkovsky was much more intense than that paid to any of the other human rights issues that have arisen in Russia in the post-Soviet period, and senior representatives of foreign governments made an explicit link between the proceedings and Russian oil production. Even U.S. secretary of state Condoleezza Rice publicly criticized Russia for prosecuting Khodorkovsky—yet in the same breath she asked Russia to ease restrictions on foreign investment in the Russian oil and gas sector, claiming that Russia was underperforming as an energy producer at a time of rising oil prices.[2]

Resource Nationalism

When oil prices are low or when high risk is involved in an exploration project, states offer foreign and private companies attractive conditions to invest in their energy resources and to take the risk on themselves. However, when oil prices are high over extended periods of time, states often become emboldened and reduce or remove the participation of foreign or private companies in energy exploration, production, or export. They adopt a policy of resource nationalism, and take advantage of their newly acquired power under tight oil markets to attempt to revise agreements with foreign energy companies, nationalize energy industries, and advance state ownership of energy resources.[3]

In the framework of the resource nationalism policies, states often recapture profits made in the initial production and export periods by foreign and private energy companies by altering the interpretation or implementation of tax codes to allow collection of back taxes. In addition, governments often change tax regimes to recapture profits made under the existing agreements between the state and the private or foreign enterprises.

Resource nationalism policies usually make little economic sense, since they tend to harm production and export capabilities and thus ultimately state revenues. Substituting state oil companies for foreign and private partners often means less efficient operation and more limited access to advanced exploration and production technologies. These policies also hurt the climate for future foreign and private investment in the states. As stated by William Ramsay, deputy director of the International Energy Agency, "The rise of nationalism is a concern for future (oil and gas) production."[4]

In most cases where governments nationalized their oil industries in the 1970s or tightened the fiscal terms during the latest round of tight oil market conditions, production has sagged or even declined. Neither Libya nor Iraq has increased production in decades; Iran's production is still lower than during the years before the 1979 Islamic Revolution, and until 2006 Saudi Arabia had not increased its output in more than three decades. More recently, output from Venezuela has fallen and that from Russia has stagnated, despite the tremendous surge of recent oil revenues that could have provided resources to accelerate production. As Ramsay remarked, "They are embarking on a dangerous path. . . . Look at the production capacity of Venezuela—it has fallen dramatically. This is the price to be paid. If you don't get the balance right between the companies' interest and the country's interest, the country ultimately will lose."[5]

In Russia, resource nationalism policies that former president Vladimir Putin put into place have included the destruction of Yukos, increased taxation of exploration, and crippling the ability of most foreign energy companies to implement their contracts in the oil and gas sector in Russia. The result has been a slowdown in the growth of Russian oil production. In 2005, Russian oil production grew by only 2.3 percent, compared with 9 percent in 2004 and 10.7 percent in 2003.

Since Hugo Chávez took office as president of Venezuela in 1999, oil production levels have not recovered to those before his reign. Venezuela enacted policies in the late 1990s that aimed to increase the production share of Petróleos de Venezuela, S.A. (PDVSA), the national oil company. By 2005, not only had the country's total oil production declined by 800,000 barrels per day from its pre-1998 level, but PDVSA's production share had also fallen. Bolivia nationalized its energy in June 2006. In June 2007, another Andean country, Ecuador, established a committee to review existing exploration and development contracts in the oil sector involving private companies, indicating a plan to reopen these contracts.

States sometimes claim environmental justifications for their resource nationalism policies. This rhetoric resonates well domestically and often internationally. Libya has used this claim a number of times in its dealing with foreign companies. In 2003, Kazakhstan used environmental claims as a basis for renegotiating existing contracts with a number of major oil companies. Four years later, in 2007, Kazakhstan again used disputes over environmental policies to challenge the framework of ENI's operation of the Kashagan field. Russia has fallen back on environmental policy claims to remove Shell from the Sakhalin II natural gas production project and recapture it for Gazprom.

Energy Windfalls and Foreign Policy

During periods of high oil and gas prices and thus windfall profits, energy exporters often conduct a more assertive foreign policy, increasing their regional and at times international involvement. Indeed, their energy and political interests can overlap, with oil exporters initiating crises that lead to further oil price hikes.

Venezuela has attempted to endow itself with a leadership role in Latin America and the Caribbean by offering subsidized oil and gas shipments to its neighbors. The country now sells oil to clients in the Caribbean Sea at a 40 percent discount from international rates. In addition, in April 2007, Chávez offered leftist states in the region a 50 percent discount, stating that Venezuela intends to "put its oil reserves at the service of Latin America."[6] Chávez also aims to build a gigantic pipeline—stretching more than 5,000 miles—that will supply most of South America with natural gas from Venezuela and Bolivia. The Venezuelan leadership admits that the pipeline is guided more by political than by economic logic. Ángel González, general director of exploration and production at the Venezuelan energy ministry, stated that "It's not that the economic part doesn't matter, but it's really not the most important part of this project."[7]

Beginning in 2003, the power of the ruling regime in the Islamic Republic of Iran increased due to the rising oil revenues that began to flow into the government treasury. Tehran's foreign policy in this period was also progressively emboldened during the crisis between Iran and the International Atomic Energy Agency over its nuclear program. In 2004, conservatives gained control of parliament after thousands of reform-minded candidates were disqualified by the regime on the eve of the election. In June 2005, Mahmoud Ahmadinejad was elected president of Iran. His election symbolized a dramatic shift in Iran's foreign policy rhetoric, and to the adoption of a more confrontational Iranian foreign policy.

During periods of tight oil market conditions, producers often take foreign policy actions or initiate crises that serve both their foreign policy agendas and their energy interests, since these crises generally cause oil price spikes. Among these dual uses of crisis is an event in March 2007, when Iranian forces took British sailors hostage. This action deterred foreign forces from coming close to Iran's contested maritime borders, put pressure on the United States in its holding of Iranian agents captured in Iraq, and led to an immediate 9 percent jump in oil prices that was sustained for a number of weeks. This jump included the biggest one-day price rise since December 2001. In addition, during a visit to ideological ally Nicaragua, Venezuela's Chávez stated openly his policy of pushing up world oil prices: "Oil is going straight to $100; no one can stop it."[8]

High oil revenues also give oil producers funds that can be used to finance terrorist activities. Some Middle East producers, such as Saudi Arabia, provide funding to school systems and terrorist groups that work against ruling regimes in the Middle East, in hopes that this will shield them from activities to overthrow their governments.

The "Oil Weapon"

In periods when the international oil market is tight, there is generally a surge in commentary on the perceived use of oil or energy as a weapon.[9] In discussions in Washington and in Europe, legislators and policymakers debate ways to abate the danger of the oil weapon.

Is there an energy weapon? Can producers deny energy supplies to a state or group of states to achieve political goals or weaken an opponent? In addressing these questions, it is important to differentiate between the dynamics of natural gas and oil supplies. As discussed in Chapter 1, the nature of natural gas supply is fundamentally different

TABLE 1. Major Oil Producers and Exporters

Major oil producers	Percentage of world total
Russia	12.4
Saudi Arabia	12.3
United States	7.9

Major oil exporters	Million tons
Saudi Arabia	358
Russia	248
Islamic Republic of Iran	130

Sources: International Energy Agency data, 2006 (exporters), 2007 (producers).

from that of oil supply. Oil is a fungible commodity that is traded on international markets. In contrast, natural gas is supplied generally in bilateral frameworks between the supplier and the consumer, and due to logistical limitations that limit opportunities for supply alternatives, is more subject to political influence. Because of these differences, this chapter will treat oil and natural gas separately, first focusing on the possibility of an oil weapon and then discussing the role of politics and the impact of supply disruptions in the sphere of natural gas supplies.

Since the oil market became global in the late 1960s, there have not been successful instances in which suppliers imposed an oil embargo on consumers. Specific countries cannot be denied supplies unless all producers participate. If certain producers decide to halt sales to a specific country, other producers will supply the targeted country, and in the end all consumers will bear the brunt of the price increase spurred by the so-called embargo.[10] However, through declarations and threat of supply cuts, major oil exporters can cause price spikes and shocks without any change in the concrete supply situation. A successful example of this policy is Iraq's and Iran's April 2002 threat to halt oil exports for a month in solidarity with the Palestinian people. The two states did not obstruct or cut the flow of a single barrel, but oil prices soared in response to the declarations.

The potential impact of a threat or actual denial of oil supplies by an exporter generally depends on the state of the international oil market. The most infamous incident of the attempted use of an "oil weapon" was the 1973 OPEC oil embargo. This attempt at imposing an embargo on the United States and the Netherlands, which triggered a quadrupling of world oil prices in a short period, was preceded by other declared embargos (1956, 1967) that had an inconsequential impact on the world oil market. The previous embargos had taken place when the oil supply market was saturated. However, under tight oil market conditions, removal or threat of removal of even a small amount of oil can significantly affect world oil prices. Prior to the October 1973 boycott attempt, a significant decline in U.S. spare capacity oil production had resulted from underinvestment, caused by the preceding decade of low oil prices. These tight market conditions allowed the declaration of the OPEC oil embargo following the 1973 Arab-Israeli war to significantly affect oil prices that were already on the rise.

Despite the sustained tight oil market conditions in the early twenty-first century, the major industrial states are less vulnerable to the price surges and spikes caused by threat of supply disruptions then they were in the 1970s. Today the United States and Europe use half the amount of oil per dollar of GDP produced that they did in the 1970s.[11] In addition, following the 1970s oil crises, the United States and other OECD member states established oil supply stocks that help cushion the blow during periods of potential oil price surge and reduce fears of supply disruptions. Moreover, the major oil exporters are much less prepared to sustain extended export disruptions than in the past, with their economies increasingly dependent on oil revenues. Those oil exporters with large populations supported by the oil revenues, such as Iran and Venezuela, are particularly dependent on continuing high exports.

The threat to wield the oil weapon has had mixed economic results. In the short run, calls for export disruptions have often led to immense short-term economic gain for the exporters. The 1973 embargo, while reducing world oil supply by only 5 percent and lasting for only two months, generated tremendous revenue gain in the year following the declaration. However, following 1974, OPEC inflation-adjusted oil revenues declined each year by approximately $50 billion.[12] OPEC also lost a large portion of its market share to non-OPEC producers in response to the declared embargo in the 1970s, from 53 percent at the time of the boycott to around 35 percent today.[13] Moreover, the embargo encouraged consumers to substitute natural gas, nuclear energy, and other fuel sources for oil. During the time of the boycott, oil made up 45 percent of the world energy mix; today it stands at 35 percent and is in decline.[14]

Despite frequent rhetoric to the contrary, the oil trade seems to reflect few nationalist and religious sentiments. Countries in conflict often trade in oil indirectly. For instance, Israeli refineries receive oil from Middle East countries with which it is formally in a state of war. Despite the adversarial rhetoric aimed at the United States by Venezuela's Chávez, South American producers deliver nearly all their oil exports to the United States. Even though it serves as the security guard for most of the oil-producing states in the Persian Gulf, the United States imports significantly less oil from the region than Europe in both absolute and relative terms, and the Middle East supplies oil chiefly to Asia. Russia and the Caspian states deliver most of their oil to Europe and Mediterranean countries, dictated chiefly by geographic proximity between the suppliers and the markets.

While oil supply embargos by producers have been an infrequently used and very ineffectual tool, embargos on investment in the oil and gas sectors have been imposed on a large number of oil and gas producers. In the last two decades, many oil exporters have been the target of both U.S. and UN Security Council sanctions (Iraq, Iran, Sudan, and Libya). The large investment necessary to develop oil and gas is an obvious target for sanctions on energy exporting states.

The Gas Weapon

Since natural gas began to be used on a widespread basis, there have been few cases of politically motivated natural gas supply interruptions. Many of the interruptions were initiated by the consumers and the transit states, and few by the suppliers. One of the most remarkable cases of gas supply disruption initiated by a supplier was Algeria's policy in the early 1970s. This series of disruptions was intended to increase the price of its sales by pipeline and liquid natural gas (LNG). Algeria did not have an overt political motive in the supply cut. Algeria's gas wars cost it dearly: in the short run, while its LNG facilities were not used, and in the long run, as it took decades to overcome its reputation as an unreliable supplier.

The nature of natural gas supplies makes this fuel much more susceptible to political considerations than oil. In contrast to oil, which is traded primarily on international markets with little connection between the supplier and the consumer, natural gas is supplied chiefly in pipelines, creating direct, long-term linkages between suppliers and consumers. The high cost of natural gas transport infrastructure requires and creates long-term supply relationships between parties. The relationships impact and are impacted by political factors. This section will discuss the interplay between political factors and natural gas supply relationships. Specifically it will address the questions: Are gas importers dependent on the suppliers, or does interdependency develop between the sides? Under what conditions is an importer dependent and on which is there interdependency between the sides? How does the natural gas supply relationship impact the political relationship between the sides? How does the potential availability of LNG impact the nature of existing gas supply relationships?

TABLE 2. Major Natural Gas Producers and Reserves

Major natural gas producers	Percentage of world total
Russia	21.5
United States	18.0
Canada	6.0

Major natural gas reserves	Percentage of world total reserves
Russia	27.2
Iran	15.3
Qatar	14.6

Sources: International Energy Agency data, 2007 (producers); 2008 (reserves).

Some Basics on Natural Gas Supplies

Natural gas consumption has seen a significant increase since the 1970s; its share of world energy consumption is the fastest growing and is expected soon to overtake coal as second in world total consumption. Natural gas's main constraint is the difficulties in its transport: it can be moved by pipeline or in liquefied form (LNG) by special tanker. Due to the high costs of production and transport of LNG and the cost and limited number of facilities, only a quarter of international natural gas trade is in that form. Unlike oil, which is traded on an international market, natural gas supplied in pipelines is generally traded in the framework of long-term contracts.[15] LNG is traded in a mixed manner—some in long-term contracts between producers and consumers, and some on international markets.

Again in contrast to oil supply dynamics, which allow states to import from a wide variety of sources and quickly find new sources of supply on the open global market, states rarely have options of diversifying their natural gas supplies or creating multiple parallel supply mechanisms to enhance their energy security. Logistical limitations of natural gas supplies include the high costs of investment and long-term nature of payback, as well as the time needed to establish and construct an international natural gas pipeline. These factors prevent commercial entities from deciding to join a market that is already supplied: rarely will a commercial entity decide to become the second natural gas supplier to a market. In addition, because the high costs and long-term nature of the planning generally will benefit only future generations (and, more important, future voters!), governments only infrequently support the cost outlays involved. Because of the lack of commercial or government interest, states rarely have multiple gas supply infrastructures.

New international gas transport pipelines need to operate for at least fifteen to twenty years before investments can be recouped. Accordingly, interested investors and linked governments assess the prospects for long-term operation of the pipeline, including the stability of the involved states. These inherently political assessments even affect the price tag of the projects, since funding costs will be much higher if the project is viewed as politically risky. Therefore, participating states and companies make great efforts to ensure positive political and security relations before undertaking a major energy transport project that links them. In addition, investors scrutinize the political orientation of the involved governments, such as their commitment to the free market and rule of law, in order to protect their investments.

Nonetheless, after an energy infrastructure project is initiated, countries often continue to joust about the terms of operation and the distribution of revenue. Testimony to these efforts is the fact that government affairs departments are typically among the most central units in major energy companies.

The continued quarreling over the terms of international infrastructure export projects results from two factors. First, the relative bargaining power of the various parties changes once major investments have been made in a project. While trying to court an investor or attract a transit route, a country may offer attractive terms. But once the investor has actually put money into a project, much of the negotiating leverage is lost. After all, once constructed, there will be no use for such facilities other than to export the energy of the supply state, which can then dictate new terms to the supplier.

Second, most major oil and gas reserves are located in nondemocratic states. If a regime change occurs in such a state, previously negotiated contracts are typically not honored. Moreover, pursuit of an agenda to gain larger revenues for the state provides a populist method for the new regime to establish its legitimacy.

Dependence or Interdependence?

As noted, because of the expense of building natural gas supply infrastructures, states rarely possess multiple infrastructures. Thus in theory they are dependent on suppliers, and are potentially vulnerable to the supplier taking advantage of that dependency to for political and security goals. Consumers are not in a position to make quick shifts in their supply options. Their only option is potentially to alter the fuel source— for instance, to substitute coal or oil for natural gas when producing electricity. Accordingly, energy consumers and supply states linked in long-term natural gas supply relations are often interdependent: the consumer for supplies, the supplier for a market.

When suppliers and consumers are interdependent, the gas supply between them is generally stable and less vulnerable to political and security ebbs and tides. Whether the relations are dependent or interdependent seems to depend on a number of factors: symmetry in the level of dependence of a supplier and a consumer (which is often connected to the size of the market in question) and the extent to which each has alternative supply or market options, including transport infrastructure.

In theory, all natural gas importers that lack extensive alternative import capability, such as extensive LNG import capacity, are potentially at risk for supply disruptions and accordingly dependent on their suppliers, rendering them vulnerable to the dictates of the supplier state. In principle, one could view the EU, which will soon be importing a third of its natural gas from Gazprom, as dependent on Russia's supplies and potentially vulnerable to Moscow's dictates. However, since it lacks alternative export infrastructure at this stage, Russia is also dependent on the European market.

At the same time, in assessing the extent of dependence and potential vulnerability to the gas weapon, one must look at both the short and the long term. In the short term, the cost of lack of supply is much higher and more dangerous than the cost of lack of payment for supply. Thus during times of crisis between states or when regimes may be focusing on short-term goals, the importing states are more vulnerable than the exporters, even if the market is of great importance to the exporter. German energy expert Friedemann Müller described the potential vulnerability of Germany in the hands of Gazprom: "The asymmetry of dependency can be seen in the fact that temporary delivery interruption could have catastrophic economic and social consequences for the consumer, while a temporary refusal by the consumer to pay for deliveries would not have the same impact on the supplier."[16] At the same time, states and regimes that would like to be long-term suppliers must take into consideration their reputation for reliability. However, some regimes may think more of short-term gain or personal interests, and not necessarily the good of future generations.

The anticipated world rise in the use and supply of LNG will reduce supply vulnerability in many short-run situations. At the same time, almost counterintuitively, extensive access to LNG adds an element of instability in long-term natural gas supply relations. As noted earlier, the stability of long-term supply relations is affected by the symmetry of dependence between the supplier and the consumer and the existence of alternative transport infrastructure. Extensive LNG export or import capacity creates an alternative transport infrastructure. If both sides

TABLE 3. Top Five LNG Exporters

Qatar
Malaysia
Indonesia
Algeria
Nigeria

Source: International Energy Agency data, 2007.

have this capacity, their supply relations are in constant negotiation, since supplies can be obtained or exported through this alternative. If only one of the sides has extensive LNG capacity, then this side will possess the power in the relationship and the nonpossessor will be more vulnerable. Thus, while LNG capacity will enhance short-term supply and export options for natural gas, in the long run LNG use will make gas supply relations more unstable and can upset the interdependency of states in such a relationship.

Security of Markets

Just as energy exporters seek diversity of supplies, natural gas exporters aspire to acquire diversity of export markets. It enhances their security for export options and also increases their ability to bargain successfully for higher prices for their exported gas. Exporters will always prefer direct routes to consumers versus options through transit states, even if indirect routes are less costly in the construction stage of the project. In the last decade, Russia has sometimes spent exorbitant sums to diversify its export routes to Europe, just to reduce its dependence on transit states. This policy will have a significant impact on its relations with these states.

While energy suppliers and consumers are cautious in their denial of supplies or markets, transit states are more likely to be tempted to use their role to elicit economic, security, and other gains. As a result, supply arrangements that have transit states in between the supplier and the consumer are less stable than direct ones. In the past decade, the world has witnessed a number of crises and developments that testify to the importance of energy transit states in the security of energy supply. However, this is a risky business for transit states; such action can spur investment in more direct routes between suppliers and consumers.

Although some transit states at times enact policies of threatening obstruction to transit as a means to elicit better economic terms or another material outcome, the transited state covets this role and generally does not want to lose it. Thus there generally is a limit to the extent that it will threaten transit. Poland, for instance, strives to maintain its role as a transit state for Russian oil and gas in order to deter Moscow from attempting to impose its will on Warsaw in a variety of spheres. Iwona Wisniewska of the government-sponsored Center for Eastern Studies in Warsaw noted that "once the North European Pipeline was built, Poland would lose its status as a transit country for Russian natural gas exports to Europe and a bargaining chip with the larger country."[17]

In addition, exporting states, while not enjoying their vulnerability to supply disruptions, recognize that transit can be an important carrot in their relations with transit states. In the 1990s, Moscow used the transit carrot effectively with neighboring Baltic states, even playing them against each other to offer Moscow better conditions to retain its transport facilities in their respective states. Once Russia stops using transit routes through these states, it will also lose a tool for influence in them.

Similarly, energy transit states can receive significant policy benefits because of their role. An important example is the relationship between Azerbaijan and Georgia. The transit relationship with Azerbaijan was made possible after the states had entered a string of cooperative relations in a variety of spheres, including security. Georgia's president Mikhail Saakashvili pointed out, "Our success is Azerbaijan's success and vice-versa."[18] Both states had become pillars in NATO's Partnership for Peace program and both adopted strong security orientations toward the United States prior to the emergence of the transit frameworks. Accordingly, not only is the transit via Georgia very stable, but both sides have made important concessions to increase each other's stability and prosperity, assessing their mutual dependence and benefits from the transit relationship. Azerbaijan, for example, supplies gas to Georgia at extremely low rates. Moreover, Azerbaijan is footing the bill for Georgia's section of a railway being built from Azerbaijan to Turkey through Georgia. Furthermore, Baku invests significant policy efforts to ensure that the sizable Azerbaijani minority in Georgia are complacent and does not undertake any policy agendas that could be destabilizing for Tbilisi. Baku and Tbilisi have both demonstrated prudent and conciliatory policies in their border delimitation agreements. In 2007, the two sides agreed to share a monastery on a border site claimed and revered by both nations as a means to prevent potential conflict between the states.

While serving as a transit state can provide certain economic and political benefits, the role can also make a state more vulnerable to destabilization measures by states vying for power in a region. An important example is Russia's attempts for over a decade to destabilize Georgia. Tbilisi is a special object of Moscow's policies in the region, precisely because its geographic location provides it with the pivotal role of providing a transit route for the landlocked states of Central Asia and the Caucasus. One of the means Moscow uses to destabilize Georgia is support for the secessionist enclaves of South Ossetia and Abkhazia. Moscow's desire to undermine Georgian attempts to provide transit for Central Asian natural gas to European markets was a factor in its August 2008 attacks on Georgia under the guise of supporting the South Ossetian breakaway region.

Ironically, despite suffering from transit difficulties itself, Russia is a very shrewd transit state that exploits the vulnerability of the landlocked energy producers in Central Asia to an unprecedented degree. Moscow has retaken control of some of the main gas transport infrastructures in Central Asia. By preventing access to foreign markets without crossing Russian territory, Moscow also maintains crucial leverage over these states. They are forced to sell their natural gas to Moscow, which exports it to the European market at twice and sometimes three times the purchase price from Central Asia. During 2006, for instance, Russia created obstacles to oil exports from Kazakhstan through its territory via the Caspian Pipeline Consortium (CPC) pipeline, the only oil pipeline in Russia outside the full control of the Russian state company Transneft. Moreover, since most of the regimes in Central Asia are relatively unstable and vulnerable, the Russian government often uses its ties with competing elements in the regimes (and potential elements that can destabilize the regime) to pressure Central Asian producers to conform whenever they try to pursue export options outside the Russian-controlled infrastructure. Moscow took advantage of the vulnerability of the regime changeover in Turkmenistan following the death of President Saparmurat Niyazov in December 2006 and the internal coup attempt by President Nazarbayev's son-in-law in Kazakhstan in June 2007 to deter these regimes from exporting their natural gas resources through routes other than Russia.

Energy Weapon or Commercial Considerations?

In the winters of 2006 and 2007, a string of crises between Russia and the bordering former Soviet republics resulted in temporary energy cuts to those now independent states. Georgia and Ukraine claimed that Moscow tried to punish them for their Western orientations and color revolutions that had removed regimes that were accommodating to Russia's demands, and to use the gas weapon to destabilize their regimes. Moscow claims that its disputes with these states and with Belarus are commercial: it cannot continue to sell oil and gas to former Soviet republics at prices far below alternative markets in Europe and beyond. In truth, Moscow's policies in the crisis with Belarus and Ukraine were motivated by a combination of these and other goals. They included gaining control of neighboring states' transport and distribution systems for economic gain and political leverage over former Soviet states, altering their transit practices, and commercial considerations. In the case of Georgia, the timing and the abrupt nature of the supply cuts were also determined by political considerations.

The supply and transit relations between Russia and the former Soviet republics are exceptional. Generally, good political relations and cooperation precede the building of linkages in major energy infrastructure projects. The infrastructure that links Russia and the former Soviet republics was built as domestic Soviet pipelines, and the supplies flowed on a noncommercial basis. The new states were accustomed to not paying for energy from Russia; at the same time, Moscow was accustomed to having control of the export infrastructure and Central Asia's natural gas volumes. Initially after the Soviet breakup, there were no mechanisms to measure the amount of gas and oil consumed by the neighboring states and their corresponding debts to Moscow. Disputes over energy supplies and transport and transit arrangements fed into the larger task of untangling and institutionalizing the relations between the new states that once were part of a unified state. Until 2005, most of the former Soviet republics that received energy from Russia paid subsidized prices. In 2005, Gazprom announced that its gas customers in the former Soviet republics should pay alternative market prices for its gas. This was applied to both close allies like Armenia and Belarus and adversaries like Georgia.

In addition to bringing oil and gas supply prices closer to those in other export markets, Moscow strove to gain control of the energy transport and distribution networks in neighboring states for long-term economic gain and leverage over the policies of the neighboring states, and to prevent the energy producers among them from circumventing export through Russia. In 2003, the Russian government published *Russia's Energy Strategy Until the Year 2020*,[19] which openly declared that one of Moscow's policy goals was to regain control of energy transport and distribution networks in neighboring countries, including reuniting the electricity grid in the former Soviet space. As part of this policy, Moscow has tried both carrot and stick. Gazprom offered moderately priced energy supplies with only gradual increases to neighboring former Soviet republics that surrendered control over their energy infrastructure. States that have refused to sign over their infrastructure, such as Azerbaijan and Georgia, were forced on January 1, 2006, to immediately pay the same prices as European customers or abruptly lose supplies during the winter.

Transit is also part of the winter energy crises. Since the Soviet breakup, Ukraine and Belarus have been problematic oil and gas transit states for Russia. Throughout the 1990s, both states regularly siphoned off energy supplies intended for European markets, and have not regularly paid their energy bills, even for supplies at subsidized rates. On the eve of its winter crisis, each country conducted brinkmanship policies with Russia with the goal of attaining better terms for their energy supplies, each banking on the fact that Moscow is dependent on the two states for its exports to Europe. In contrast to suppliers that are wary of tarnishing their image as reliable suppliers, Ukraine and Belarus knew that if supplies were disrupted, Moscow, not the transit states, would pay the price in terms of its image. Thus, the two countries calculated that their behavior was not overly risky for them. Moreover, it seems that in Ukraine and Belarus the central governments do not have complete control over the behavior of a number of economic and government entities, which often pursue policies for short-term personal gain, without considering the long-term implications for the state.

Moscow called the bluffs of both Ukraine and Belarus, and cut gas supplies to Ukraine in winter 2006, and oil supplies to the Druzhba pipeline through Belarus in winter 2007. Consequently, both sides incurred losses: Europe began to question its deepening dependence on Russian gas supplies and explore diversifying its imports, while both Ukraine and Belarus landed worse financial terms than they had before the crisis. In addition, Ukraine is more dependent than before on Russia. As part of the resolution of the crisis, the two sides established a shadow Russian Swiss-registered company called RosUkrEnergo to handle Turkmenistan's gas supplies to Ukraine, ending Kiev's access to an additional supplier.[20] In light of the crisis, both Russia and its partners in its vital export market in Germany have accelerated their efforts to build a direct gas pipeline link between them under the Baltic Sea, circumventing the current pipelines through Ukraine and Belarus. Hardly four months after the Belarus supply crisis, Gazprom announced that it had lined up funding for the trans-Baltic pipeline in partnership with the German firm E.On, which, incidentally, is the largest foreign holder of Gazprom shares.

In the case of Gazprom's gas cuts to Georgia in winter 2006, the timing and the manner had explicit political goals, in addition to the economic agenda pursued vis-à-vis all the former Soviet republics. The gas cut to Georgia coincided with a cut-off of electricity supply from Russia that Moscow dubiously claimed resulted from terrorist attacks on the line. The simultaneous cuts of gas and electricity supply plunged Georgia into darkness and cold during perilous winter conditions. Clearly, if Moscow's policy goal was purely commercial, it could have delayed the gas cuts until the electricity line was repaired out of humanitarian concern. Moreover, in the post-Soviet era Russia has had a history of using the energy weapon to attempt to pressure Georgia to change its policy stances. Since Mikhail Saakashvili's ascent to power in Georgia on the heels of the October 2003 Rose Revolution, Moscow has timed the disruptions to undermine Saakashvili's attempts to stabilize the country. In the winter of 2007, Gazprom raised prices to Azerbaijan and threatened to cut its gas supplies when Baku offered to supply Georgia with energy in anticipation of another supply cut from Russia. Georgia's vulnerability to Russia's use of the gas weapon was significantly lowered in 2007 with the commencement of gas supplies from Azerbaijan through the South Caucasus pipeline (SCP).

Historically, Georgia had been an easier target than Ukraine and Belarus for Moscow's use of the gas weapon. Unlike those two states, Georgia has not been a transit state by which Moscow reaches important gas markets. Russia's line to Georgia only continues to the neighboring small markets in the Caucasus: Armenia and Azerbaijan. Thus, Georgia did not have a lever to counterbalance its dependence on Russia in the sphere of energy. In addition to the political disputes, in the past decade the two states have sparred over Georgia's bills to Russia, including Moscow's charges to Tbilisi for energy supplies to the breakaway region of Abkhazia, which has been under Moscow's de facto control since 1992.

Lessons for Energy Security

Moscow's natural gas crises with its neighboring states spurred Brussels and Washington to think hard about Russia's reliability as an energy supplier. Western Europe's experience with Russia as an energy supplier has been very different than that of the former Soviet republics: Moscow has been a major natural gas supplier to Europe for more than 30 years with no intentional supply disruptions; political ebbs and ties have not had any influence on the energy exchange. The supply relationship between Moscow and Europe has even tranquilly endured the transition from the Soviet Union to Russia. Due to the relative symmetry of dependence between Moscow and Europe, the potential supply vulnerability of the countries of Western Europe is much lower than that of the former Soviet republics. Russia's dealings with its former Soviet neighbors are not necessarily a model for Russia's future gas supplies to Europe.

States that have no counterbalance to the energy weapon are vulnerable to its use. States with small markets that are considering imports from Gazprom should heed the lessons from these cases, especially Moscow's use of the gas weapon to promote political goals in Georgia. Israel, for example, is considering contracting major gas imports from Gazprom via Turkey, and could become vulnerable if Russia were to use the energy weapon to promote its policies in the Middle East.

At the same time, Europe should draw the lesson from the string of energy crises that Moscow takes European natural gas demand for granted. Russia was not afraid to tarnish its image as a reliable supplier to Europe when it cut its gas supplies to Ukraine and oil supplies to Belarus, leading to minor changes in its supply capability to Western Europe. Generally, major energy suppliers are extremely cautious in taking any action that could hurt their reputation for reliability, an important precondition for receiving additional investment funds in energy production and export infrastructure. In response to the crises and Europe's concerns about Moscow's reliability in light of the energy cuts to the former states, Gazprom managers responded tartly: "We want European countries to understand that we have other alternatives in terms of gas sales. We have a fast growing Chinese market, and a market for liquefied natural gas in the U.S. If the European Union wants our gas it has to consider our interests as well."[21] Accordingly, Moscow made no efforts to court Europe and allay its fears after the string of crises, further illustrating that it takes European natural gas demand as a given.

One can draw the conclusion that the real competition for energy resources is not between the United States and China but between Europe and China. If Russia were to build export infrastructure to China, Russia's natural gas supplies might not easily meet the combined demand, and the competition between them would put Moscow in a good bargaining position with regard to both.

Another lesson from Russia's energy wars with its neighbors is that states will not always act in their own best interest. Generally, neither major natural gas exporters, major markets, nor transit states will want to upset their supply relations. However, as we have learned in the last string of crises, a considerable amount of money is at stake in energy exchanges and none of the sides operate as unified actors. Thus, personal short-term interests within a state often set policies more than overall long-term interests of the state. Supply relations will always be vulnerable to potential interruptions as long as someone stands to gain from them. Consequently, in analyzing supply relations, it is important to remember that rational decisions will not always prevail.

Another lesson to be learned from analysis of Russia's energy is that Russia and Iran are natural competitors in natural gas supply. Iran is the only country with the volume and location to pose any major threat to Russia's dominance in Europe and some of the markets in the former Soviet Union. In spring 2007, Moscow at great expense and policy maneuverability bought out Iran's potential access to the European gas market through Armenia. In the unfolding developments over Iran's nuclear program, policy-makers should keep in mind this rivalry between Russia and Iran in the sphere of natural gas supplies.

Chapter 3
Pipeline Trends and International Politics

Different means of energy transport create varying relations between suppliers and consumers and have differing political ramifications. In the twenty-first century, new trends have emerged in energy transport that have immense political implications: pipelines are reemerging as a major means of energy supply. In its early production period during the last quarter of the nineteenth century, oil was transported primarily by pipeline, train, and barge. After World War II, tankers at sea for the most part replaced pipelines for oil transport. Consequently, pipelines are used today to transport only a small portion of oil trade: two-thirds of the world's oil trade is transported by tankers.[1] Tanker transport allows flexibility and frequent changes in destination for both suppliers and consumers and is much cheaper than pipeline transport. The shift to tankers allowed oil markets to become truly global; for most of the second half of the twentieth century, oil was sold on world markets, and direct contact was not required between the producer and the consumer. In contrast, energy pipelines link suppliers and consumers in a long-term relationship, require long-term investment, are highly vulnerable to security threats, and are directly affected by the political relations between the linked states. Most oil pipelines in use today transport oil within states (including to domestic ports to be transported by tankers to international markets); few are international.

Natural gas, unlike oil, is not easily or economically transported by sea vessels, and thus most international supplies are through pipelines, linking producers and consumers. Until the late twentieth century, however, natural-gas use and export occupied a modest portion of world energy consumption.

Beginning in the twenty-first century there has been a significant increase in two forms of energy pipeline transport: pipelines directly linking producers and consumers and multiple-state oil transport entities. The rise in such pipelines has occurred because of three major factors: the dramatic increase in global use of natural gas; the rise in production and export of oil and gas from landlocked states (high oil prices rendered such production commercially viable); and the breakup of the Soviet Union, which shifted the supply of oil from Russia to Eastern Europe to a commercial rather than a "fraternal" basis even as it used the direct pipeline infrastructure in place between the former Soviet-era allies.

This trend is likely to continue. Sustained high oil prices and increased world demand for oil, as well as the desire of a number of consumer states that a larger portion of these volumes will come from non-OPEC member states to increase world energy security, will lead investors and developers to energy volumes in complicated locations—geologically, geographically, and politically.

Pipeline Trends

The means used to transport energy and the degree of direct linkage—or lack thereof—between producer and consumer affect energy security options and political relations. As noted, for most of the second half of the twentieth century, oil was the major source of energy trade, and it was traded on international markets, with few cases of direct physical supply between producers and consumers. This fact reduced the impact of politics on specific oil-trade deals and the potential use of oil supply to advance political goals with a specific consumer.

During this period, most pipelines were used merely to transport oil within a state or from production locations to ports. Only a few major international oil pipelines were in operation, and many of those had been built when the connected states were part of a larger political entity. Some remained from the British Mandate in the Middle East, and from the connections between former Soviet republics and allies. A few also connected states with very limited coastal access, such as Iraq, with ports in other countries.

At the beginning of the twenty-first century, a number of new international oil pipeline projects have emerged, including direct oil supply pipelines and projects for the export of oil from landlocked countries. These projects usually involve substantial volumes of oil, given that the new generation of pipelines is wider. And they involve substantial technical and financial challenges, which virtually require the extended involvement of international energy companies. Since these projects are capital intensive and have a long payback period—typically fifteen to twenty years or longer—investors have a strong interest in the political stability and orientation of the involved states. But the involvement of these companies and the need for stable diplomatic relations to maintain support for such pipelines lead to their own characteristic types of politics.

Direct Linkages

International oil pipelines that do not lead to world markets but directly link producer and consumer were until recently quite scarce. But today some have been established and new ones are under consideration—for example, by Russia to China and by Venezuela to a number of neighboring states. Pipelines are becoming more attractive, in part, as a means to circumvent major maritime chokepoints and congested waterways, often due to security or environmental considerations.

Still, direct oil supply between producer and consumer leads to increased opportunity for the states to influence each other's politics. (These types of direct relationships between energy supplier and consumer were previously only seen with the supply of natural gas.) The impact of these direct supplies on the world oil market is not clear. Under existing projects, oil is supplied at varying world market rates. However, conceivably, in supply relations in which the oil cannot reach world markets, bilateral prices may be set, similar to the mechanism of natural gas supply.

The two major direct oil supply pipelines in operation are the Druzhba pipeline from Russia to former Soviet allies and republics and the Atasu-Alashankou pipeline from Kazakhstan to China. During the Soviet era, the Druzhba pipeline supplied oil to Russia's East European allies on a noncommercial basis. Following the Soviet breakup, the operating principles of the pipeline changed dramatically, and consumers are now charged prices more in line with world oil prices. Druzhba, which began to deliver oil in 1962, is the longest oil pipeline in the world, 2,500 miles (4,000 kilometers). It pumps 1.2 million barrels a day to Eastern and Central Europe, with one arm running to Poland and Germany and the other to Ukraine, Hungary, Slovakia, and the Czech Republic. The centrality of the Druzhba pipeline to world oil markets was illustrated in July 2006, when the pipeline's spur to Lithuania broke, causing an oil spill and suspension of supplies to Baltic Sea ports. This incident forced an immediate and extended spike in world prices, with a greater long-term impact on prices than the military confrontation that took place also in summer 2006 between Israel and Lebanon's Hezbollah.

Some transit states have complicated the flow of oil along the Druzhba in recent years by linking passage to the state of agreements with Russian gas giant Gazprom on gas supply tariffs. For instance, in the winter of

2007, oil supplies in the Druzhba were interrupted because of a conflict between Belarus and Russia over how much Gazprom should pay Minsk for transit fees in its annual contract.

Nonetheless, Russia is likely to build additional international energy pipelines in the near future. Russia has few ports that are operational year-round, and these are far from many of Russia's major oil sources, making pipeline options relatively attractive.

The Kazakhstan-China Oil Pipeline

In December 2005, the Atasu-Alashankou section of a pipeline between Kazakhstan and China was inaugurated. This stage of the pipeline is 625 miles long and cost $806 million. It annually supplies 70 million barrels (10 million tons) of oil from Kazakhstan to China. The volumes transported are modest in this first stage, but the two countries plan to increase the pipeline's capacity and lengthen it on both sides of the border. At completion, it should be able to supply 140 million barrels annually. The pipeline is a fifty-fifty joint venture between the state companies China National Petroleum Corporation (CNPC) and KazMunai-Gaz. CNPC is not only a partner for the pipeline, but also the major investor in the oil field, Kumkol, which is the source of supply for the first stage of the pipeline. Oil is sold through this pipeline on a fluctuating price basis, based on world oil prices.

The pipeline has generated interesting local cooperation and ties. On the Chinese side of the pipeline, an oil refinery and petrochemical plants are budding, built around Kazakhstani oil supplies. In addition, direct commercial ties seem to be expanding between the populations on both sides of the border. The pipeline links Kazakhstan with China's Xinjiang autonomous region. The political implications of this may be significant, since the region is populated on both sides of the border primarily by ethnic minorities, most of Muslim background. Many of the residents in the border area share ties with co-ethnics on the opposite side of the border, such as members of the Uyghur nation.

Both countries had strong political motives for establishing the pipeline. Kazakhstan seeks multiple routes for its energy exports in order to lessen its dependence on a single or small number of transit states. Today, Kazakhstan's oil is imported through Russia, and Moscow has proven to be a problematic transit state. The country also exports small amounts of oil in swaps with Iran, and is considering exporting additional volumes through the Baku-Tbilisi-Ceyhan pipeline. Although the cases are still few, this pattern appears typical of many landlocked states. Azerbaijan also aspires to export its energy by multiple pipelines, albeit the modest volumes discovered so far have failed to produce a basis for multiple transit routes. Kazakhstan, a landlocked state nestled between two great powers—Russia and China—conducts a foreign policy of accommodation with its neighbors and seeks to build mutual dependencies. Kazakhstan hopes that the pipeline will spur additional trade and ties between it and China. At the pipeline's inauguration, president Nursultan Nazarbayev predicted that the project would "double the trade between Kazakhstan and China."[2] From Beijing's perspective, the direct oil supply pipeline fits its current energy security policy by providing access to oil that is not dependent on transport on international seaways.

Landlocked States: Multistate Energy Transport Projects

Energy export projects that are multistate, lengthy, and expensive and that in previous decades might have been considered outlandish are almost commonplace today. Sustained high oil prices and increased natural gas exports have rendered projects of this type commercially viable, and a policy desire to offset the power of OPEC producers has given impetus to such oil pipelines.

Since the 1990s, a number of major oil and gas production and export projects have been launched from the landlocked countries of Kazakhstan, Azerbaijan, and Chad. Investors previously had overlooked these locations because of the higher price of extraction of oil from them than from those with global ports. Moreover, during the Soviet period, Moscow preferred to invest in oil production in other locations, mainly in Russia itself. The Soviet breakup and high oil prices have rendered oil production in landlocked states commercially attractive. That means that more borders will be crossed in the supply of energy than in the past. There are two important geopolitical consequences: the formation of groups of states linked together by major infrastructure projects and the enhanced importance of energy transit states in regional and international political systems.

The linking of states in international energy supply relations expresses a willingness to forge interdependency between them. Projects of this type are generally preceded by significant strategic cooperation. Moreover, the two sides, once in the interdependent relationship, take measures to nurture its stability. For instance, Baku invests significant policy efforts to ensure that the sizable Azerbaijani minority in Georgia is complacent and does not undertake any initiatives that could be destabilizing for Tbilisi. Moreover, Baku and Tbilisi have both demonstrated prudence and compromise in their border-delimitation agreements. In 2007, the two states even agreed to share a monastery on a border site claimed and revered by both nations as a means to prevent conflict between them. The strength of the political relationship between the sides influences and is influenced by the cooperation on energy. Azerbaijani president Ilham Aliyev has remarked in the context of the Baku-Tbilisi-Ceyhan pipeline that "Energy cooperation leads to regional cooperation."[3]

For major energy infrastructure projects, many commercial and political considerations cannot be neatly detached and are often interrelated. The price of building infrastructure such as pipelines is affected by the political risks involved and the investment environment. Thus, states in choosing routes for the export of their commodities and the importation of their energy supplies naturally consider the political ramifications of various route options. Once invested, they seek to ensure that their investments are protected by maintaining stable relations.

Landlocked states have special interests in the stability of their transit and port states and in attaining influence in those states. As Kazakhstan's Prime Minister Karim Massimov put it, "One of the highest priorities of Kazakhstan is the stability of Georgia."[4] Subsequently, in 2007, Kazakhstan became Georgia's largest foreign investor. Azerbaijan also offers Georgia low-cost gas supplies to loosen Tbilisi's dependence on Russia and strengthen its ability to conduct independent policy.

Linking states in oil and gas infrastructures often paves the way for additional infrastructure links. Other infrastructure links run along the line of the Baku-Tbilisi-Ceyhan pipeline and the South Caspian pipeline, which transports natural gas. These include electrical connections and a railway project. Other economic ties in nonenergy and transport sectors are developing between the states as well as frequent exchanges between the citizens of the involved countries. Moreover, multiple-state entities, like the Baku-Tbilisi-Ceyhan (BTC) pipeline project, demand enhanced political and security cooperation spheres and become the basis for expanded joint efforts in these fields.

As previously indicated, in long, multistate energy transit projects, the political relations between the parties become paramount to their success. We can see why export projects from landlocked countries thus generate increased political involvement by interested states and international institutions. This is illustrated by examples in this chapter of the BTC and the Chad-Cameroon pipelines. Before commercial investors agreed to participate in the BTC, there was an unprecedented amount of political activity that won the project extraordinary backing from the U.S. government, thus reducing some of the risk involved in implementing the project. The Chad-Cameroon pipeline was established with the help of extraordinary involvement of the World Bank.

Some believe that the multinational nature of these projects makes them more stable, even though they are more complex in their composition. William C. Ramsay, deputy executive director of the International Energy Agency, believes that the multinational character of these new pipeline projects enhances their viability: "The more flags that are planted in a pipeline, the harder it is to cut off."[5]

Case Studies of Two Pipelines

The BTC pipeline project became operational in spring 2006, and the Chad-Cameroon pipeline project did so in 2003. The BTC pipeline illustrates the unique policies of landlocked energy exporters, the quest for exporters to choose suitable transit states, and the nexus of political and economic interests in the establishment of major multiple-state energy-export projects. The Chad-Cameroon pipeline also involves a major landlocked energy-export state, Chad, which is linked with Cameroon, which has an Atlantic coastline. The uniqueness of this case is the extensive involvement of an international institution—the World Bank—in a pipeline's establishment and operation. Through the BTC various states attempted to promote political goals in parallel with Azerbaijan's export of oil; for the Chad-Cameroon pipeline, the World Bank attempted to promote its agenda in the sphere of governance and poverty eradication through the energy-export endeavor. This project also illustrates the unique cooperation and convergence of interests between an international economic development organization and an international oil company in the development of a major oil production and export project.

The history of both pipelines shows that multiple state projects of this nature take a long time to establish. Putting the extensive funding in place and building sufficiently stable political relations between the export and transit states in order to reduce risk is a time-consuming process. Each of the projects took over a decade from the period of the initial decision to export oil through the designated transit states and the actual operation of the pipelines.

The Baku-Tbilisi-Ceyhan Oil Pipeline

The BTC pipeline is important for understanding some of the current dynamics of international energy politics. When the pipeline opened for operation in 2006, it defied the pessimistic assessments of energy experts, journalists, and many non-U.S. policy-makers who had dismissed it as being both unable to attract commercial investment and unrealistic from a political and security perspective.[6] The pipeline transports oil from the Azerbaijani section of the Caspian Sea on an east-west route over a distance of 1,087 miles (1,750 kilometers), similar to the distance from New York to Miami, and cost more than $3.6 million. The

BTC is the second-longest oil pipeline in the world, after the Druzhba pipeline. It crosses three countries, entailing complicated legal frameworks and extensive coordination. The pipeline supplies a million barrels per day—a little over 1 percent of the world's daily oil consumption. Kazakhstan intends to join the BTC pipeline and export part of its expanding production volumes through the pipeline, thus extending the scope of the project. Parallel to the oil pipeline runs a natural gas pipeline—the South Caspian pipeline, or "Baku-Tbilisi-Erzerum"—which became operational in 2007.

Project Background

Since antiquity, Azerbaijan has been known as a source of oil and natural gas. Fire worship rituals related to the flames that were known to jump out of the earth in this area are a central part of the ancient pre-Islamic culture of Azerbaijan and still a prevalent cultural motif in the land. Azerbaijan was one of the most important centers of oil production in the late nineteenth century. At the end of that century, it supplied more than half the world's oil. During the Soviet era, Azerbaijan's energy riches were not intensively developed, with Moscow preferring to invest in developing the energy riches in Russia itself, due to both strategic and technological considerations.[7] After the Soviet breakup and the independence of the republic of Azerbaijan in December 1991, the new state sought to develop its oil and gas resources. As a landlocked country, its export options were complicated by the need for a transit state. Transit options included south to Iran, north through Russia, and west through Georgia and Turkey.[8] Baku had hoped to build multiple export pipelines to offset its dependence on one transit state, but the volumes discovered in the state did not justify more than one pipeline. President Heydar Aliyev decided that the main export pipeline should be built on an east-west route, through Georgia and into Turkey, and primarily led by Western oil companies. Aliyev made this strategic decision for two major considerations: he wanted the pipeline to go through a country friendly to Baku and one that would allow Azerbaijan to have sway over it, reducing Baku's vulnerability to transit stoppage. Accordingly, Georgia was the most attractive transit option. In addition, Aliyev viewed the east-west export infrastructure as an opportunity to join other U.S. strategic frameworks, a goal that was desirable in light of his perception of the United States as the world's leader. In explaining his strategic decision, Aliyev remarked to his close foreign policy adviser, Vafa Quluzade, "the Kremlin is now in Washington."[9] In contrast to the conclusions of many academic analysts, Baku did not relinquish the Iran option because of pressure from Washington; rather, the Heydar Aliyev government never seriously entertained the Iranian route.[10]

Figure 1 The Baku-Tbilisi-Ceyhan and Baku-Tbilisi-Erzurum pipeline routes.

In the early 1990s, Washington also actively promoted export of Azerbaijan's energy along an east-west corridor. Contrary to popular myths, Washington was not interested in gaining control over Azerbaijan's modest energy volumes, but rather saw the energy transit route as a tool to foster security and political ties with the Caspian states. Those in high-level U.S. policy circles believed that if Azerbaijan's energy resources were transported to market through Russia or Iran, Baku would not be able to adopt a pro-Western security and political orientation. Bill Richardson, secretary of energy in the Clinton administration, stated the U.S. approach quite clearly:

We're trying to move these newly independent countries toward the West. We would like to see them reliant on Western commercial and political interests rather than going another way. We've made substantial political investment in the Caspian, and it's very important to us that both the pipeline map and the politics come out right.[11]

In 1994, Azerbaijan signed the "contract of the century" with BP, Amoco, and other U.S.- and European-based oil companies, setting the stage for foreign long-term involvement in energy export projects in Azerbaijan. A 1999 NATO summit in Istanbul was another important milestone in the progress of the BTC pipeline. Azerbaijan, Georgia, and Turkey signed a transit agreement, and the United States played a key role in securing the pact. Nonetheless, BP (which became the main operator of the pipeline project) only set funding for the undertaking in place in 2001, and the inauguration of the project did not take place until 2005. The BTC pipeline became fully operational in spring 2006, more than a decade after Baku made the strategic decision to export its oil by this route, illustrating the principle that projects of this complex nature require a long period of political nurturing until they can be realized.

Implications

The BTC pipeline strongly illustrates that major energy infrastructure projects inherently involve political considerations, both international and domestic. Despite the relatively modest volumes of oil in the Caspian Sea, the pipeline's construction was preceded by an incredible amount of political activity by the project's proponents and opponents. Several heads of states took a stand, and the route and funding of the pipeline entered U.S. congressional debates, where a number of ethnic-based lobbies—led by Jewish, Turkish, and Armenian lobbies—actively campaigned for and against the undertaking. President Clinton personally endorsed and promoted on a number of occasions, making it one of the rare overseas energy infrastructure projects on which the president of the United States has taken an official stand.

Many opponents of the Baku-Tbilisi-Ceyhan pipeline dismissed it by declaring that the route was "political," stating that market forces alone should determine the routes of energy transport and that Washington should not take policy stances on energy infrastructure projects.[12] Nonetheless, the United States, Russia, and Iran all vied to have Caspian oil and gas exported through their territories or, in the case of the United States, through states fully affiliated with the Euro-Atlantic alliance (Turkey and Georgia). The modest volumes of oil and gas in question, in contrast to the colossal political efforts the competing sides invested to promote and thwart various pipeline options, indicate that the pipeline route was to be used as a means of influence in cementing a new geopolitical order in the Caspian region. The states that attempted to determine the route of the export of Caspian oil were interested not primarily in potential transit tariffs, but in the political influence transit states would be granted over the landlocked Caspian area. Accordingly, Washington supported an east-west route through states allied with it in Euro-Atlantic security structures in order to grant Azerbaijan and other states the opportunity to orient themselves toward these alliance structures. In parallel, Washington sought to encourage development of energy sources outside OPEC and Russia in order to increase world energy security through diversity of sources. Secretary of Energy Richardson stated, "This is about America's energy security, which depends on diversifying our sources of oil and gas worldwide."[13]

Furthermore, Washington sought to increase the political influence of NATO ally Turkey in Central Asia and the Caucasus and boost Turkey's fledging economy, which had been damaged by the lack of oil exported through its territory from Iraq since the end of the first Gulf war in 1991. In addition, Washington was eager to support energy projects that did not pass through the environmentally and safety sensitive Bosporus Strait, a position that Turkey actively promoted in Washington.

Through the BTC pipeline and other Caspian infrastructure projects, Washington sought to reduce the dependence of regional states on Russia. However, it was not a U.S. goal to exclude Russia from energy infrastructure projects in the region. Evidence that Washington was not attempting to push Russia out of the region can be found in U.S. support for the Caspian Pipeline Corporation (CPC) project, which exports oil from Kazakhstan through Russia. The CPC was the first major and most expensive energy export infrastructure that the United States supported for export of Caspian energy. In contrast to U.S. policy toward Russia, from its beginning the first Clinton administration implemented policies aimed to keep Iran from gaining significant influence over the new Caspian states. Starting in 1996, with congressional enactment of the Iran-Libya Sanctions Act (ILSA), Washington's policy also included active opposition to any major Caspian energy projects that had major Iranian participation or that transited Iran. Of course, as indicated earlier, Washington did not have to persuade Baku to adopt its position that its oil should not transit through Iran: Azerbaijan did not seriously consider exporting the bulk of its energy resources through a neighboring country with which it had tense relations.[14]

Baku's decision to export its oil through Georgia and Turkey instead of Iran or Russia illustrates the principle that energy-exporting states prefer to transit their energy sources through states with which they maintain friendly relations, and if possible, are weaker than they are. The exporting state is thus less vulnerable to transit stoppages by the transit state.

The case of the BTC also illustrates that energy-export states make significant efforts in order to ensure the stability and vitality of their neighboring transit states. In the case of Azerbaijan and Georgia, both sides have undertaken significant policy steps to ensure the stability of each member of the transport pair. For example, during the negotiation process over transit agreements, World Bank experts applied significant pressure on Azerbaijan to increase the price it would charge Georgia for natural gas from the South Caucasus pipeline that would transit Georgian territory. Baku strongly resisted the World Bank proposals, preferring to ensure Georgia's economic viability and thus increase its stability.[15]

The BTC case throws light on the interplay in Washington between domestic considerations and foreign energy policies. U.S. policies toward the Caspian region states, specifically those toward energy pipeline routes, have been influenced throughout the 1990s and into the first decade of the twenty-first century by intense political activity by various U.S. ethnic-based lobbies. Since the eve of the Soviet Union's breakup, Azerbaijan and Armenia have been in conflict over the Nagorno-Karabagh region. Subsequently, the Armenian American lobby has promoted a number of congressional initiatives aimed to thwart U.S. aid to Azerbaijan and investment in the east-west pipeline.[16] Additionally, this lobby attempted to convince Washington to try to coerce Baku into building its major export pipeline through neighboring Armenia. The Armenian-American lobby convinced a number of U.S. congressional representatives to actively promote nonsensical legislation aimed to force Azerbaijan to export its natural resources through a country with which it was at war. In contrast, lobbying groups aimed at aiding Turkey actively supported the Baku-Tbilisi-Ceyhan project as a way to bring investment to Turkey and further cement Turkey's role as a vital component of U.S. policy in the region. Jewish political groups, interested in reducing global dependence on oil produced in Arab countries, actively supported the BTC pipeline in Congress and with the executive as a means of developing non-OPEC energy sources. Additional motives were fostering ties with and cooperation between Israel and the moderate Muslim-populated post-Soviet Caspian states and strengthening Israel's de facto alliance with Turkey. The impact of these lobbies' activities on congressional positions on issues related to both the pipeline and wider U.S.-Caspian regional policy led to reversals and inconsistencies in U.S. policy. Consequently, Washington's ability to be effective in the region and to earn the full trust of the leaders and publics of the Caspian states was compromised at times.

In analyzing policy stances in the Caspian region, it is necessary to separate those of the U.S.-based energy companies and those of the U.S. government. Despite Washington's support for the BTC project, few U.S.-based companies took a role in the project. In fact, today few oil companies in Western countries act in concert with the governments of their home countries and often distance themselves. London-based BP is the largest stakeholder in the BTC and also the operator of the project. Other large stakeholders are the State Oil Company of the Republic of Azerbaijan (SOCAR) and Norway's Statoil. It should be noted that the major U.S. energy companies active in the Caspian region did not support Washington's promotion of the east-west corridor pipeline, and that most of the major investment in the project is from non-U.S.-based oil companies.

The business-driven agendas and policies of the Western oil companies (and some of the Russian oil companies as well) set them apart from most of the Middle East and most other OPEC member oil companies, which are national oil companies and operate as an arm of the government. The geographic home of the different companies is not symmetric to the policies of their home governments. Among BP's goals in leading the project was to use it as a framework to increase long-term cooperation with the U.S. government, and to ensure its primacy in the Turkish energy market. In addition, the assets of the companies are located in a variety of global locations, not necessarily overwhelmingly in their home countries.

The Chad-Cameroon Petroleum Pipeline Project

The Chad-Cameroon oil export pipeline is a unique international energy infrastructure project. As part of its funding structure, Chad agreed to place the majority of the oil revenues generated by the pipeline under international scrutiny and regulation. As part of the framework, the funds were to be used to eradicate poverty and promote public good. The Chad oil revenue program was considered a model program for other oil and resource producers. A World Bank expert remarked, "it is an extraordinary, and was at the time, virtually unique, start among oil dependent developing or transition countries. It will be watched closely by all countries and institutions concerned with the management of petroleum reserves."[17]

This project is the most extreme intervention of an international financial institution in a country in an attempt to circumvent the resource curse and democracy deficit of major oil exporters. The project saw unprecedented involvement of an international institution in an energy export project. Through involvement in this project, the World Bank and a number of international oil companies partnered in the establishment of the framework and in the recruitment and provision of the funding, along with managing this major oil production and export project. The Chad-Cameroon pipeline is an example of the increasing activism of international institutions and the extension of this activism to unprecedented spheres of activity—such as the establishment of oil export projects and pipelines. It shows the role international institutions can play in mitigating risk involved in potential production and export projects, thus making them more viable for investment. In both the policy community and academic circles, there was great hope that through the outside intervention the development model in Chad would succeed and contribute to peace and the welfare of the citizens in that country.[18]

Chad's special developmental challenges and its relationship with its chosen transit state, Cameroon, are typical of the policy challenges confronting landlocked energy producers. As a landlocked state, the export of oil from Chad demanded not only investment in exploration and production in its oil fields, but a transit pipeline to bring the oil to port for transport to world markets. Thus, the project demands higher investment than export of oil from sea abutters and a durable framework of cooperation between Chad and its outlet to the sea, Cameroon.

Project Background

International oil companies first discovered oil in Chad in the early 1970s in the Doba and Lake Chad basins in the country's south. Civil wars, accompanied by external interventions that raged in the late 1970s and 1980s, delayed development of Chad's oil resources. The year 1988 was a landmark in the development of Chad's oil: a consortium of international oil companies, led by Exxon, signed an agreement for an oil exploration license that was valid until 2004.[19] By 1993, significant oil resources were confirmed in Chad's Doba region. Because it is a land-locked country, it was necessary to establish a transit framework to export Chad's oil. Accordingly, in 1996, Chad and Cameroon concluded a bilateral treaty for the construction and operation of an oil export pipeline through their territories. Two national pipeline companies were established in 1998 to construct and operate the pipeline: Tchad Oil Transportation Company S.A. and the Cameroon Oil Transport Company S.A. (COTCO). The project is operated by a consortium comprised of ExxonMobil, Petronas (Malaysia), and ChevronTexaco.

In the late 1990s, the World Bank began to take an active role in the contours of the project, including funding. Its contribution to the funding comprised $93 million in loans from the International Bank of Reconstruction and Development (IBRD) to finance Cameroon's and Chad's participation in the project, $100 million in direct loans from the International Finance Corporation (IFC) to the oil consortium, and $300 million from commercial banks raised by the IFC. While the actual financial participation of the World Bank was not large, its involvement in the project eased efforts to raise funds. In the words of Donald R. Norland, U.S. ambassador to Chad from 1979 to 1981, the bank's participation served the role of "risk mitigation."[20] While it is not clear whether the World Bank's involvement in the project was at the Bank's initiation or that of the main participating companies, the investors welcomed and encouraged it to undertake an active role.

According to its statements, the World Bank took the role to ensure that revenues from oil extraction would be used to benefit the people of Chad, specifically for poverty eradication. According to an official statement, the "World Bank saw this as a unique opportunity for Chad to climb out of extreme poverty."[21] The bank conditioned its participation and the granting of loans to Chad on its implementation of a revenue management plan. Accordingly, in 1998 Chad approved a law setting out the government's poverty reduction objectives and arrangements for the use of oil revenues. Under the law, 10 percent of Chad's direct oil revenues (dividends and royalties) were to be held in trust for future generations; 70 percent were to be allocated to health, education, rural development, environmental concerns, water resource management, and other social services. The law also established an independent oversight committee to approve and monitor spending. The committee is comprised of Chadians from various sectors of society, including representatives from the Supreme Court, parliament, a local NGO, and a trade union representative. In parallel, the World Bank set up and financed an international advisory group to guide the project. This group was to have unrestricted access to documents and personnel.

Despite this legal arrangement, Chad violated the terms as soon as it

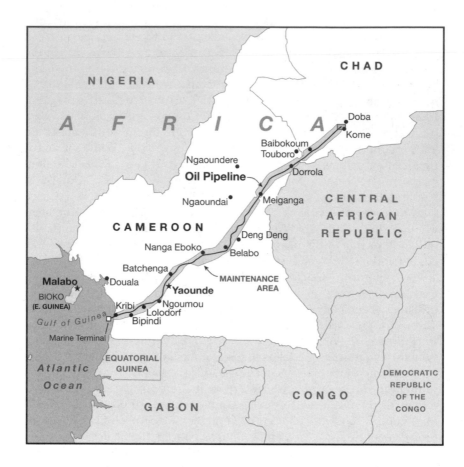

Figure 2. The Chad-Cameroon pipeline.

received its first payment—a \$25 million signing bonus marking the project's groundbreaking, which it used to purchase weapons. The arms purchase sparked disagreement between the World Bank and the government of Chad, with the Bank noting that the purchase was made with the approval of Chad's parliament.[22] A major crisis between the sides broke out in January 2006, when the government of Chad decided to alter the terms of the agreement. Chad's parliament voted to change its law in order to allow the disbursements to be used for military purchases and to double the percentage of the funds that could be spent by the government without stipulations. In response, the World Bank suspended its loans to Chad for the project.

In response to the World Bank action, Chad's finance minister Abbas Mahamat Tolli said that

> It is unacceptable that a nation should have its access blocked to revenues generated by the sale of its own natural resources. Chad's government will take appropriate action to recover the legitimate rights of the Chadian people. . . . The oil revenue will be used for the welfare of our youth instead of being put aside for future generations as the World Bank wants us to do.[23]

Implications

Despite the fact that in recent decades few underdeveloped countries have succeeded in improving their economic and governance plight through energy extraction and export, international development and financial organizations and many academics continue to advocate this route to poverty-stricken countries. In the case of Chad, the World Bank took on itself an unprecedented role in mobilizing funding and in managing revenue, believing that with its involvement in the project, the recipe for circumventing the resource curse could be found. Even before the project yielded any of the desired results, the Bank and other project proponents presented the Chad-Cameroon pipeline project as a model illustrating that resource extraction can play a positive role in alleviating poverty and establishing health, education, and other social welfare programs.[24] For example, in April 2002, on the eve of commencement of the flow of oil along the pipeline, the U.S. House of Representatives International Relations Subcommittee on Africa held a hearing entitled "The Chad-Cameroon Pipeline Project: A New Model for Natural Resource Development." Despite these attempts and the strong belief in the project, the case has failed to produce results that differ from the patterns of other oil producers in underdeveloped countries.

While the project has failed to guarantee that the oil revenues generated will be used to eradicate poverty and for the general benefit of the people of Chad, the project framework did interject transparency into the revenue use. The terms of the Chadian legislation were changed openly and approved by the parliament. The international advisory group makes regular field visits to Chad and Cameroon and publishes findings on the environmental and social impact of the project. Moreover, financial transparency received a boost through monthly publication of the consortium's royalty payments to the escrow account of the government of Chad in London and the disbursement of those funds to Chad.

The case of the Chad-Cameroon pipeline, like the BTC, shows that energy export from landlocked countries is especially complicated and difficult to realize. From the time of the conclusion of the interstate agreements between Cameroon and Chad and the agreements between the government of Chad and the main investing companies, led by Exxon, and the actual operation of the project, close to a decade elapsed. Like the BTC, the pipeline project was very expensive, costing $4.2 billion.

The complexity of the export of oil from landlocked countries and the need to build a stable political framework with the transit state seems to invite outside intervention in projects of this nature. Moreover, since export of oil from landlocked states requires higher risk and investment than most oil extraction and export from sea abutters, the investing companies welcomed the involvement of an external actor like the World Bank that could help mitigate their risk.

Transit States

With the increasing internationalization of the oil and gas trade, rising consumption of natural gas, and initiation of the export of oil and gas from landlocked states, energy transit states are emerging regionally and in the international system. Their role affects their strategic value and position. Georgia is particularly illustrative: by using its geography to forge an important energy transit role, states can carve for themselves an important geopolitical role.

The main potential value of achieving a role as a major energy transit state is geopolitical, since transit is not especially lucrative financially for the transit states. As noted in this chapter, Georgia and Cameroon are slated to earn the modest sum of approximately $500 million over the next 25 years for the transit of energy export through their territories. Moreover, states that are trying to position themselves as transit states undertake large financial risks. Turkey, for instance, has signed agreements for more natural gas imports than its domestic market can consume, with hopes of exporting this gas to other markets. However, the main supplier of gas to the Turkish market, Gazprom, has not granted Turkey a re-export license for its gas and no firm commitment for a consumer or investor for export infrastructure has been found. Moreover, transit fees, like oil sales revenues, tend to be collected by the states and produce little economic growth.

Chapter 4
Conflict

The drive to control oil and natural resources is frequently said to be a cause of wars between states and within states. Former U.S. secretary of state Henry Kissinger warned that the global battle for control of energy has become a major source of conflict: "competition for access to energy can become the life and death for many societies."[1] As we saw earlier, U.S. senator Richard Lugar, an elder statesman on foreign policy issues, views conflict over energy as a major source of future confrontations. He has called for NATO to alter Article Five of its charter so that energy embargos against a member state would be considered an attack on the alliance. "In the coming decades," Lugar notes, "the most likely source of armed conflict in the European theater and the surrounding regions will be energy scarcity and manipulation."[2] A long list of academics and pundits claim that competition for control of scarce energy resources will be a major source of conflict in the twenty-first century.

Clearly, during wartime control of oil and other energy resources is part of the strategic aims of each combatant in order to sustain the war effort and in order to deny one's adversaries access to vital supplies. Since Winston Churchill in 1912 led the British Admiralty to adopt oil-powered ships, and the subsequent building of armies based on oil-consuming vehicles, regular access to oil has become a precondition for conducting modern warfare. The birthday cake Hitler's generals gave him in 1941 that was shaped like the Caucasus—and of which Hitler took at bite out of Baku—is a vivid and chilling symbol of the importance of oil riches in war. Moreover, the prevailing types of energy in use have a significant impact on the types and distances of wars states can fight. An excellent example of this principle is the effect the introduction of nuclear-powered submarines had on the dynamics of global nuclear deterrence.

However, the role the drive to control oil and energy plays in spurring interstate wars or in intrastate conflict is far less clear. The thesis that competition for access to energy serves as a source of armed conflict between states rests on the assumption of scarcity of supplies or future supplies. Yet no such scarcity exists: the market has continued to stay ahead of demand. Moreover, in a globalized oil market, possession of oil sources does not mean that a state is adversely affected by world price trends; thus, access to oil does not insulate a state from the economic threat of high oil prices. In addition, in times of conflict a state must possess not only access to external energy sources but the ability to transport that energy across vast distances. In a globalized world energy market, the idea of "controlling" access to energy sources abroad is antiquated, especially if a state does not have the military capability to actually exert its access to the resource.

At the same time, the drive by most states to exploit additional energy resources is a growing source of border-delimitation conflicts. Until recently, many disputed borders areas—especially in the sea—have been left undetermined, since there was no concrete need for delimitation. However, with the discovery or the potential existence of oil and gas resources in many of these disputed zones, border-delimitation conflicts are emerging in a number of locations between states, especially in Asia. Key areas of contention and potential contention are the Caspian Sea and the Arctic Circle.

There is no concrete evidence that energy supply relationships contribute to the alleviation of conflict. As seen in the previous chapter, peace and good relations between exporting and transit states and consumers must precede the decision to build a pipeline. In cases where the infrastructure was built prior to the establishment of cooperative relations (under colonial rule, for example), the inherited infrastructure can serve as a source of tension, and not promote peace.

Interstate Conflict and Cooperation

In a series of publications, Michael Klare has promoted the idea that at some point in the near future supplies of petroleum will not meet demand, there will be not be a viable energy substitute, and the world will encounter significant energy shortages, leading to the emergence of conflicts between states for control over resources. Writing in his book *Resource Wars*, Klare argues that

Unless some plentiful new source of energy has been discovered by that point, competition over the remaining supplies of petroleum will prove increasingly fierce. In such circumstances, any prolonged interruption in the global flow of oil will be viewed by independent states as a mortal threat to their security—and thus a matter that may legitimately be resolved through the use of military force.[3]

Some specialists take issue with this view of access to energy as a potential source of conflict. Robert Manning, for example, argues that "the whole notion of a world of resource scarcity which energy security defined in nineteenth-century neo-mercantilist terms of competition for territory and diminishing oil reserves is not the world of the first quarter of the twenty-first century."[4] Foreign investment in oil and gas production and export projects does not guarantee that the resources will arrive in the investing state. Much of the oil produced by national foreign energy companies is not necessarily equity oil—oil that belongs to the producers, but instead sold on international markets. In addition, partnership or ownership of energy sources abroad does not guarantee they can arrive home. Importing states, regardless of the legal status of oil they would like to import, need to have effective means to transport it home. Few states can challenge Washington's naval supremacy in the world's vital sea-lanes, and most are content for the United States to conduct and pay for this policing job.

Energy and Border-Delimitation Conflicts

The drive to exploit oil and natural gas resources leads to two main types of border-delimitation conflicts: sovereignty in an area whose status is disputed that contains or potentially contains oil or natural gas resources, and distribution of the rights to extracting an energy resource that transits a number of borders.

A vast number of the world's border areas have not been delimited. This is especially true for countless maritime borders. Many states dispute the borders between them, but have left the issue unresolved, since there was no practical need for the delimitation. However, once one of the countries involved in a border issue begins the exploration and production process, the issue tends to move to the forefront. High energy prices and growing world demand have made many areas of interest commercially that were previously overlooked for exploitation due to their geographic, geological, or geopolitical complexity. And many of these are found in areas of contested sovereignty between countries. In the last decade, a number of direct military confrontations have emerged between states attempting to survey or exploit oil or gas resources in contested areas.

In addition, oil and gas deposits that cross frontiers also create a unique set of challenges to the states that share the deposit. In contrast to mineral deposits, where the dividing line of the deposit is separable into clearly defined units, oil and gas deposits that extend beyond a dividing line can be exploited, wholly or in part, from either or both sides of the line.[5] In the case of liquid deposits shared by two or more states, division is especially complicated, because no state can determine the precise amount of oil or gas that it owns, and the situation demands cooperation from all the involved states. Moreover, exploitation by one of the involved countries affects the state of the deposits and their accessibility by the other countries along the line.[6] Consequently, traditional principles such as sovereignty over natural resources, sovereign rights, and territorial integrity are not applicable to the delimitation of liquid mineral deposits that overlie a number of borders. For practical reasons, therefore, affected states at times choose to cooperate in exploration and exploitation of oil and gas resources that lie in a number of states.

Future Border Hotspots

A number of areas with disputed sovereignty or through which oil and gas deposits transit a number of states may serve as future delimitation hotspots. Many of the spots that are listed below have witnessed violent confrontations in recent decades.

• *Iran-Qatar.* Iran and Qatar share the North Field/South Pars gas reserves. This underwater gas reserve contains the world's largest concentration of proven gas, with 20 percent of the world's known reserves. The maritime border of this field was demarcated in the late 1980s, but since the deposit is shared by the two states, either country's exploitation affects the access to and state of the other's deposit. Qatar has built extensive liquid natural gas facilities to export the gas from this and other fields, and is today's the world's largest LNG exporter. Iran exploits only a minor portion of the gas in its segment of the reserve, the South Pars field. In April 2004, Iran accused Qatar of overproducing its share of natural gas from the North Field and threatened that if it did not stop, Iran would resort to "other ways and means of resolving the issue."[7]

• *Iran-United Arab Emirates (UAE) disputed area.* Iran and the UAE dispute control of the islands of Abu Musa, Greater Tunb, and Lesser Tunb in the eastern corner of the Persian Gulf. The islands are especially valuable because they most likely sit adjacent to rich oil reserves, in a strategic position in the Persian Gulf from which traffic flow can be significantly affected. Iran seized Greater and Lesser Tunb from the UAE in 1971. Iran shared control of Abu Musa with Shajah (part of the UAE) until 1994, when it occupied the island. Iran now claims sovereignty over all the islands and rejects attempts to arbitrate the dispute.

Iran has increasingly expanded its military presence in Abu Musa in the last decade.

• *Spratly and Paracel Islands in the South China Sea.* Sovereignty over these islands is disputed between China and the other bordering states, Brunei, Indonesia, Malaysia, the Philippines, Taiwan, and Vietnam. The conflict between China and Vietnam is particularly robust. It is not clear that the region contains extensive natural gas or oil, but the interested countries perceive that it may and thus promote their claims to sovereignty. The region is also important to the bordering states because of the value for fishing and as a strategic sea-lane.

In the last three decades, the region has seen increasing militarization, and a number of its states have established military bases or naval stations. Fighting has erupted on several occasions. The most significant violent confrontation took place in 1988 between China and Vietnam, leading to more than 150 casualties. In 2005, China, Vietnam, and the Philippines signed an agreement for joint exploration of the disputed territory, a breakthrough that can contribute to reducing the chance of conflict in the region. Few regular principles of border-delimitation are applicable to the territory, due to the irregular coasts and numerous clusters of islands in the South China Sea.

• *East China Sea.* The border dispute in this region focuses on the islands called Diaoya by the Chinese and Senkaku by the Japanese. Japan and China have never set a maritime border between them. The islands are uninhabitable, but undersea oil and natural gas may be in proximity. Domestic politics in each state play a role in the conflict, since the islands have been the site of periodic clashes between ultranationalist groups and naval vessels from each side.

• *Gulf of Paria.* This corner of the Caribbean Sea is disputed between Trinidad and Tobago and Venezuela. In the past, Venezuelan gunboats have boarded Trinidadian oil platforms and fired on Trinidadian vessels in the area. The Gulf of Paria contains both oil and natural gas deposits.

Peace Pipelines and Interstate Conflict

As seen in the previous chapter, infrastructure projects require good relations between states as a precondition to their success. Moreover, there is no evidence that energy supply pipelines can serve as a means for peace in conflict-ridden zones. Yet policy-makers, legislators, and academics, especially in the United States, often float the idea of peace pipelines. In the 1990s, for example, a number of U.S. lawmakers and

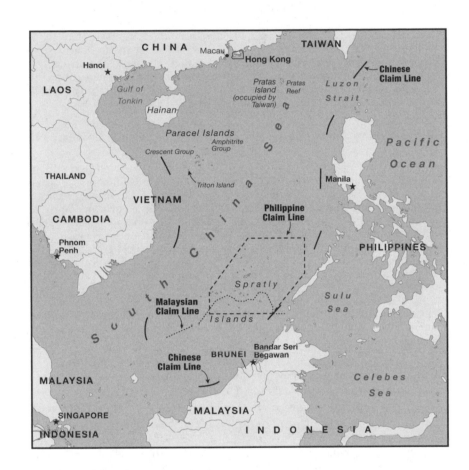

Figure 3. The South China Sea area.

State Department officials promoted coercing Azerbaijan to build its major oil export pipeline through Armenia as a means to bring peace to the South Caucasus. The former chief U.S. negotiator for the Nagorno-Karabagh conflict, Ambassador John Maresca, also frequently put forward the idea even though the two countries were at war, with their armies facing each other in a militarized and mined border and no consensus about where their border should lie. In Maresca's words,

If Azerbaijan does not seize on the possibility of building its oil pipeline across Armenia and Nakhchivan to the Turkish Mediterranean coast, it will be wasting what is a unique opportunity for ending the conflict over Nagorno-Karabakh on acceptable terms. Once a decision is made to route the pipeline elsewhere, this opportunity will be lost forever. No other possible route can offer such benefits to both Azerbaijan and Turkey. It would truly be a "Peace Pipeline."[8]

Maresca was not deterred by the state of war between Azerbaijan and Armenia:

Much of the southwestern part of Azerbaijan, where the pipeline would run, has been occupied by Karabakh Armenians for more than a year, making almost a million Azeri refugees in their own country. Nonetheless, construction could begin on the Turkish and Azeri sections of this route, with an Iranian segment in view and the possibility of adding on an Armenian segment later. . . . The possibility that a pipeline could be built across Armenia could encourage rational Armenians to join in an honest effort to find a solution to the Karabakh conflict, in order to capitalize on this unique opportunity. It will be a foolish mistake if the pipeline is not used with this possibility in mind. . . . It is also in the U.S. interest that the pipeline cross Armenia; and it is in the U.S. interest that the conflict over Nagorno-Karabakh be ended, so that the refugees can return to their homes and the peoples of the region can begin to build the positive neighborly relations which they so badly need.[9]

In addition to the unsuccessful attempts to promote a peace pipeline from Azerbaijan through Armenia, U.S. policy-makers have at times proposed a gas pipeline from Qatar to Israel to promote Middle East peace.

Iran has been actively promoting the idea of a peace pipeline to supply Iranian natural gas to Pakistan and India.[10] While clearly Tehran has significant material interest in a mega-gas market like Pakistan and India and extending its influence in these two states through the energy supplies, it attempts to explain its interest in the project as motivated by a desire to promote peace between Pakistan and India. Many have assumed that the reason the project has not materialized is U.S. pressure on India to avert a major infrastructure project with Iran. However, based on conversations with Indian officials in the energy sphere, it seems that flawed relations between India and Pakistan rather than supposed external pressure deter India from entering into a dependent relationship with Pakistan. In addition, the two sides have failed to reach agreement on the price of the exported gas. Furthermore, Iran does not produce natural gas volumes that would allow it additional exports in the near future.[11]

As shown in Chapter 3, the failure of these plans is not surprising: given the immense expense and time required for major energy transport infrastructure projects, peace and good relations between exporting and transit states need to precede the decision to build pipelines. In cases where pipelines preceded establishment of cooperative political relations, such as the situation resulting from the Soviet breakup, pipelines and transit relations often serve as a source of friction and contention between states.

An important study, *Natural Gas and Geopolitics*, examined the hypothesis that pipelines can be a mechanism to promote peace and political integration through shared economic interests. In an extensive analysis of seven case studies, along with "cursory analysis" of nearly all other cross-border gas pipelines, the authors concluded that there is "no evidence that gas pipelines are a means to peace."[12]

Like the external attempts to solve interstate conflict by linking the belligerents, Azerbaijan and Georgia had hoped that the Baku-Tbilisi-Ceyhan pipeline would contribute to resolving the secessionist conflicts that afflicted their states. But building energy infrastructures does not necessarily stabilize any of the countries along the routes, and certainly does not guarantee conflict resolution. Azerbaijan hoped that the BTC project would raise international efforts to resolve the Nagorno-Karabagh conflict with Armenia and return the secessionist region to Baku's control, while Georgia hoped its active participation would bring the international community to apply pressure on Moscow and its client separatists in Georgia to concede territories back to Tbilisi. Neither scenario became reality. Georgia's role as the major transit state of Caspian oil and gas has instead increased Moscow's interest in destabilizing the state through Moscow-backed secessionists to undermine this route that circumvents Russia.

On the flip side, major energy infrastructure projects do not need a strong security environment to become operational. Armenia and Moscow calculated that continued existence of the conflicts in the South Caucasus in which they were embroiled would serve as an obstacle to the BTC pipeline and the subsequent joining of Azerbaijan and Georgia with the Euro-Atlantic security organizations. This premise did not materialize either. Thus, we learn that pipelines do not necessarily provide the member states with a lot of stability, nor do they demand high regional stability to be established.

In addition, the BTC pipeline shows that at times oil and gas reserves can have a mitigating effect on interstate conflict. Following the return of Heydar Aliyev to power in 1993, Azerbaijan signed a painful and disadvantageous cease-fire agreement with Armenia and pursued a number of peace agreements with extensive concessions from Azerbaijan, primarily in an attempt to achieve a stable security environment to facilitate export of its oil and gas resources.

Likewise, many surmised that the symbiosis between Japan and Russia in energy interests would lead to resolution of the territorial conflict between the two countries over the Kurile Islands/Northern Territories. This conflict has lingered since the end of World War II; Japan and Russia have never concluded a formal peace treaty. Moreover, Japan imports more than 90 percent of the energy it consumes and seeks to expand its natural gas imports. Russia has extensive oil and gas reserves in areas close to Japan and seeks foreign investment and knowhow to develop these reserves. In the past decade, Japan and Russia have established extensive economic cooperation, especially in the field of energy. A number of Japanese energy companies have made large-scale investments in the development of Russia's energy resources in neighboring Sakhalin Island. Despite this increase in energy exchanges and investments, momentum for resolving the territorial conflict has shifted backward during the post-Soviet period. In both countries, domestic political opinion has tied the hands of any government that would attempt to compromise. Moreover, the leaderships' positions have moved backward from those of the early 1990s, when the two sides made great progress in the direction of resolution of the conflict.

Intrastate Conflict

In the past decade, the role of natural resources as a source of intrastate conflict has been a topic of extensive research and discussion in the disciplines of political science and international relations and among researchers and policy-makers dealing with development (especially those at international institutions such as the World Bank). The impact of energy on intrastate conflict has often been analyzed in the framework of wider studies on natural resources and conflict.[13] The groundbreaking work on natural resources export and conflict was published by economists Paul Collier and Anke Hoeffler during their tenure at the World Bank. They claim that states with more than a third of national income derived from primary commodities—natural resources and agriculture export—are more prone to civil war.[14] They argue that primary commodity dependence creates better opportunities to finance rebel groups—an important condition for conflict in the post-Cold War era. Although oil and gas are routinely included as a "primary commodity" in studies on the connection of this factor to the outbreak of conflict, it is clear that oil and gas exports do not serve as a major source of funding for rebel groups.[15] Therefore, analyzing oil and gas possession as a subset of larger studies on natural resources and conflict does not seem to be useful in understanding the specific mechanism of the impact of oil and gas on conflict outbreak.

Published qualitative analysis tends to assign a significant role to oil and gas production in increasing the likelihood of the onset of intrastate conflict, especially separatist conflict. However, the results of quantitative research on the role of oil and gas in intrastate conflict are less decisive.[16] Some quantitative studies have been published claiming that the presence of primary commodities, specifically, oil and gas in significant quantities, leads to a higher propensity for intrastate conflict.[17] But subsequent studies have shown that with small changes in the data set, the link between oil and gas and conflict can be refuted.[18] For instance, Michael Ross claims that his findings show that the link between fuel and civil war onsets was fairly robust, but after removing Russia from the data set, the correlation between fuel and the outbreak of conflict "loses its statistical significance." The dependence of these correlations on a small number of rare events should lead us to make modest claims regarding the resource-conflict link.[19] While extensive quantitative research has been published claiming that possession of oil and gas leads to higher incidence of conflict, significant follow-up research has challenged many of the studies. Moreover, the leading quantitative studies showing a statistical link between primary commodity export and outbreak of conflict attribute this link to the impact of oil and gas export on the diminished institutional capability of the state, not to a direct link between oil and gas export and conflict. In addition, many studies by the leading researchers on the topic have concluded that the causal mechanism between oil and gas export and conflict is still not clear. As stated by James Fearon, "Oil exporters do seem to have been more disposed to civil war onset, but it is not yet clear what the most important mechanisms are."[20] Despite the lack of a robust correlation in the main published studies between oil and gas possession and the outbreak of conflict, and the lack of consensus as to the mechanism and the actual link, mainstream political science publications continue to claim that the link is a given. "There is no question that oil plays a very special role in conflict," according to the authors of *Oil Wars*.[21]

In the studies claiming that oil and gas production increases the likelihood of the onset of conflict, a number of explanations are presented. Some authors have claimed that the export of oil and gas imposes on the state the characteristics of the resource curse, and that this situation makes the state more prone to intrastate conflict. For example, oil and gas can affect the tendency for conflict in exporting states since governments become less effective and more corrupt. Fearon argues that oil-producing states are more civil-war prone "because oil producers have relatively low state capabilities given their level of per capita income and because oil makes state or regional control a tempting 'prize.'"[22] Fearon and Laitin argue that oil wealth leads to state weakness, which subsequently causes civil war.[23] Ian Bannon and Paul Collier claim that rebels in oil- and gas-producing countries can attain funds to sustain a conflict by targeting the oil and gas infrastructure of foreign companies and receiving funds in return for abstaining from attacks.[24] Michael Ross claims that oil and other mineral wealth may encourage foreign parties to encourage or support a "civil war" to benefit from the fruits and future fruits of mineral wealth through intervention.[25] Macartan Humphreys argues that resource-dependent states are more sensitive to the impact of trade shocks, creating the economic conditions that make a state more susceptible to civil war.[26] At the same time, as pointed out by Ross, major oil- and gas-producing states acquire the means to fund security forces, co-opt citizens, and oppress opposition, leading to the longevity of many energy exporters.[27] Mary Kaldor, Terry Lynn Karl, and Yahia Said claim in *Oil Wars* that oil-exporting states can remain quite stable: it is only when the price falls that the capacity for patronage declines.[28]

It has been suggested that oil and gas production has been especially influential in producing secessionist conflicts, especially if the area of production is inhabited by a group with a distinct ethnic, religious, regional, or other identity. The lure of oil and gas wealth is especially useful for mobilizing a group. The consequences of oil and gas production themselves create problems—environmental, unemployment, deprivation of traditional livelihood sources, empowerment of elites—that can create or exacerbate claims and grievances of local minority groups that inhabit the production area. Oil and gas resources concentrated in a particular area of a state may foment beliefs among disenchanted groups that secession from the state is profitable and viable, whether the belief is valid or not. But oil and gas wealth in a given territory does not provide rebels with capital to finance a rebellion. Quite the opposite: an oil- and gas-rich government has the funds to better suppress a rebellion.[29] Philippe Le Billon claims that resources can motivate secessions in resource-rich regions; the distribution of benefits and externalities fueled the Biafra secession and rebellions in the Niger Delta region of Nigeria, Aceh in Indonesia, and the Cabinda enclave in Angola. He also argues that

Opposition forces operating in the context of the point and distant resources have an interest in pursuing a secessionist strategy asserting sovereignty claims over these resources. Although these resources can prove difficult, if not impossible, to access through direct exploitation, theft or extortion, their existence, or in some cases their "mythology," is a powerful tool for secessionist political justification and mobilization, while the prospect for future revenues provides an additional source of motivation. Diffuse resources, by contrast, can be more easily accessed by local populations who may, as a result have fewer incentives to confront the central government.[30]

Ross argues that resource wealth tends to promote civil wars by giving people in a resource-rich area an economic incentive to form a separate state. Using the example of the Aceh region of Indonesia, he claims that the most important source of discontent was the belief that jobs and revenues from the natural gas plant in the region were not being adequately shared with the people of Aceh.[31]

Research on the link between oil and gas and secessionist conflicts would benefit from adding geography to the analysis. While revenues from oil and gas production can serve as an effective mobilization call, many potential breakaway regions would have no means to exploit their resources without ways to export them. Moreover, active conflict areas are often unsuccessful in attracting major investment and expertise to take advantage of the resources. A number of potential secessionist groups with geographic limitations (landlocked, for example) on exporting their resources have sought revenue-sharing agreements with the central government instead of control of the energy sources and independence, recognizing the limitations to their ability to export the resources. This was seen with Tatarstan in Russia and the Kurds in Iraq.

Case Studies: The Arctic Circle and the Caspian Sea

The desire to control seabed-based oil and gas resources in the Caspian Sea and the Arctic Circle has made border delimitation in those areas particularly contentious. Most bordering states frame their claims as questions of legal rights, when in reality economics, politics, and power relations are shaping the developments in delimitations. Even international law recognizes the centrality of power to shape border-delimitation outcomes by making ownership title dependent on a state's ability to exert its control over an area.

The case of the Caspian Sea illustrates the point that oil and gas exploration and export can be conducted in areas that have no formal delimitation and sovereignty is disputed. In other words, oil and natural gas exploitation does not require recognized legal sovereignty. Some fields in the North Sea have been already depleted of their oil and natural gas resources, even though resolution of the sovereignty disputes still has not been achieved.

Arctic Circle

One of the more likely candidates for the development of a border-delimitation conflict is the Arctic Circle. Because of global climate change, in the last two decades the area of ice has receded by approximately 10 percent. The melting Arctic Circle ice has made accessible many areas that hold promise of vast quantities of oil and natural gas, as well as other minerals such as nickel and diamonds. Estimates vary as to the extent of the reserves becoming accessible in the Arctic Circle, but some place them in line with the reserves held by Saudi Arabia.

Five countries border the Arctic Circle: Russia, the United States, Canada, Norway, and Denmark. Under international law, each of the five controls an economic zone within 200 miles (320 kilometers of its continental shelf, but the exact size of that shelf is disputed. Russia claims sovereignty over 45 percent of the Arctic Ocean area, arguing that the Lomonosov Ridge is a geological extension of Russia. This underwater mountain range extends 1,240 miles (1,995 kilometers). Denmark also hopes to prove that the Lomonosov Ridge is an extension of the Danish territory of Greenland. Canada claims sovereignty over the Arctic's Northwest Passage.

The delimitation of the Arctic region and potential disputes is managed formally within the framework of the UN Convention on the Law of the Sea, the formal mechanism in place for settling disputes over exploration rights and navigational routes in international waters. All the Arctic Sea region countries except the United States have ratified the treaty. Opponents in Congress have held up ratification since 1994, claiming that the treaty surrenders too much authority to the United Nations.

Since 2006, a number of the bordering states have taken action to display their claims to sovereignty. One of the most dramatic was Russia's dispatch in August 2007 of two minisubmarines under the ice to mark the sea floor with a Russian flag. As described by a spokesman for the Russian Arctic and Antarctic research institute, "For the first time in history, people will go down to the seabed under the North Pole. It's like putting a flag on the moon."[32] President Vladimir Putin personally thanked the mission members on their return, and the newspaper *Rossisskaya Gazeta* editorialized the mission, stating that "Russia's achievement marks 'the start of the revision of the world.'"[33] In response, Peter MacKay, Canada's foreign minister, said: "This isn't the 15th century. . . . You can't go around the world and just plant flags and say 'We're claiming this territory.'"[34] Tom Casey, deputy spokesman for the U.S. State Department, was even less diplomatic in his response to the Russian expedition: "I'm not sure of whether they've put a metal flag, a

Figure 4. The Arctic Circle.

rubber flag, or a bed sheet on the ocean floor. Either way, it doesn't have any legal standing or effect on this claim."[35] A spokesman for Denmark dubbed the Russian flag anchoring "a meaningless stunt for the media."

In order to stake their claims and gather information, a number of the states in the region are beefing up their presence, including military forces. As more military vessels ply the nondelimited areas, the chances of conflict will rise. Canada has announced plans to spend $8 million to build and operate eight Arctic patrol ships in the region;[36] it has also said that it plans to patrol the Northwest Passage. The U.S. Coast Guard operates three polar icebreakers in the region, and is considering two additional ones.

Russian parliament member Andrei Kokoshin has stated that Moscow should increase its military forces in the region: Russia "will have to actively defend its interests in the Arctic. There is something to think about on the military side as well. We need to reinforce our Northern Fleet and our border guards and build airfields so that we can ensure full control of the situation."[37] In May 2007, Russia established a National Arctic Council, headed by the prime minister, designated to "develop the main directions of Russian policy to defend Russia's interest in the world's polar regions."[38]

Domestic issues could increase the chances of conflict over the delimitation of the Arctic Circle, with politicians taking up the issue to demonstrate their concern for preservation of their states' national interests. Two Russian parliament members were on board the Russian submarines that planted the Russian flag on the Arctic seabed, and it was widely covered by Russian television and other media. Parliamentarian Artur N. Chilingarov, who has taken a leading role in prodding the state to take action to assert control over the region stated after participating in the voyage that "Our task is to remind the world that Russia is a great Arctic and scientific power."[39] In addition, State Duma Speaker Boris Gryzlov praised the expedition as "a new stage of developing Russia's polar riches. This is fully in line with Russia's strategic interests. I am proud our country remains the leader in conquering the Arctic."[40]

Caspian Sea Politics

Major oil export began from the Caspian Sea began in 2000, despite continuing disagreement among the littoral states on a common principle for division and management of the sea bed or waters or delimitation of their borders in the sea. Caspian delimitation remains an open dispute that has even led to confrontation between Azerbaijani-commissioned surveyor boats and Iranian military vessels in summer 2001. Since the early 1990s, senior representatives of the Caspian littoral states have

Figure 5. The Caspian Sea area.

held regular meetings and summits to resolve the status of the Caspian Sea, with few of the meetings producing concrete results. The deliberations and conflict over Caspian Sea delimitation illustrate how political and economic interests guide legal strategies. In addition, they illustrate that oil and gas resources can be exploited and exported even in places where their status and sovereignty is disputed.

Following the Soviet breakup and the renewal of exploration and exploitation of the Caspian's oil and gas resources by the new states, conflict emerged among the littoral states over delimitation. Since the Soviet breakup, five states border the Caspian Sea: Russia, Iran, Turkmenistan, Azerbaijan, and Kazakhstan. The Caspian lacks any direct outlet to the sea; it is linked to the Black and Baltic Seas through the Volga River and a series of canals and other rivers. The Caspian is a unique body of water: it is the world's largest enclosed body of water, approximately 748 miles (1,204 kilometers) long, with a surface of 168,340 square miles (436,000 square kilometers), making it close to twice the size of the Great Lakes of North America. It is not openly navigational like the ocean, but it is composed of salt water, and it contains vast hydrocarbons unlike any other lake.

The Caspian's unique characteristics have prevented agreement on geological and legal classification. In mainstream encyclopedias and atlases, the Caspian is referred to in varying terms: a lake, a closed sea, an inland sea, an enclosed sea, a sea, and even a "unique body of water."[41] Consequently, laws governing seas and lakes do not accurately apply to the Caspian (laws on lakes refer to management of "common waters" with no guidance on the lakebed).[42]

The bulk of the Caspian's proven oil and gas reserves lie close to Kazakhstan and Azerbaijan. The sectors near Iran and Russia have not shown signs of containing considerable reserves. As a result, both Russia and Iran have directed their limited investments for developing oil and gas resources to other parts of their countries. Especially for oil, they prefer locations that have access to ports. Thus, developing Caspian energy resources is of lower priority to Moscow and Tehran than to the other Caspian littoral states.

During the Soviet period, the Caspian was divided between the Soviet Union and Iran within the framework of treaties signed between the two states in 1921 and 1940. The treaties provided for exclusive use by the Soviet Union and Iran for fishing and navigation, but do not refer to mining rights. The 1940 treaty provided for a 10-mile fishing zone extending from each side's shoreline. During the Soviet period, Moscow explored and exploited oil in the sea outside the fishing zone without formal opposition from Iran. Following the Islamic Revolution in 1979, the new Iran regime announced that it did not consider the Treaty binding, but it did not change its behavior in relation to the border in the Caspian Sea.

Since the Soviet breakup, legal positions among the littoral states have shifted in response to changing political goals and opportunities for territorial gain. After they won their independence, Azerbaijan and Kazakhstan supported dividing the sea on a sectoral basis: each state would receive a percentage of the seabed according to the percentage of shore that each possesses. Accordingly, Azerbaijan and Kazakhstan explored adjacent sectors on the basis of this formula. Turkmenistan did not possess a clearly articulated policy on delimitation and tended to sway in the direction of the policy stances Tehran and Moscow presented.

After the Soviet breakup, Russia and Iran initially presented a united position against delimitation, advocating instead a policy of common ownership of the Caspian and its seabed, prohibiting exploration of the seabed energy resources in sectors in proximity to each state's coast. As part of the "condominium" policy, oil drilling and exploration in any part of the Caspian would require approval of all the littoral states. Iran, hoping to use legal procedures to delay development of the Caspian energy resources by the new states, declared that as long as no consensus was reached on the status of the Caspian Sea, no state should be allowed to exploit the resources there. The main motivation for this initial policy by Moscow and Tehran was to ensure that the Caspian states only exported oil and gas through their countries in order to preserve their dependency. Iran was especially interested in preventing Azerbaijan from developing its oil and gas resources and thus improving its economic situation; Tehran feared that a stable and prosperous Azerbaijan could be a source of attraction to its own ethnic Azerbaijani minority, which numbers more than 20 million, approximately a quarter of Iran's population.[43]

In July 1998, a crack emerged in the united position of Iran and Russia when Moscow concluded a bilateral delimitation agreement with Kazakhstan on the seabed between them. As part of this agreement, Kazakhstan made significant concessions to Russia, including a major field believed to contain extensive oil volumes. According to a senior official who participated in the negotiations, Kazakhstan, a landlocked state, decisively relinquished those claims to the benefit of Russia, in order to achieve delimitation and thus remove obstructions to its export of the bulk of its oil in the Caspian. In the words of one of Kazakhstan's chief negotiators, "Kazakhstan decided that as a landlocked state that is dependent on its neighbors for export, it had to achieve a border delimitation agreement with Russia." He went on to note that President Nazarbayev clarified to the negotiating team prior to a crucial meeting with Russian representatives that "It is better to export oil from 90 percent of the territory we claim, than zero from 100 percent of what Kazakhstan claims in the Caspian."[44]

As part of its agreement to recognize national sectors of the Caspian seabed, Moscow won concessions from Kazakhstan and Azerbaijan that the Caspian's waters would remain in common ownership by the bordering states and that no vessels from non-abutting states would be allowed in the sea. Moscow sought support for the "divided bottom, common waters" principle to prevent U.S. naval forces from entering the Caspian at the invitation of Azerbaijan or Kazakhstan. Accordingly, Russia has delimited the border with both its neighbors in the Caspian within the framework of bilateral agreements. Azerbaijan has struck such a deal with Russia, but not with Iran or Turkmenistan. Iran has not delimited borders with any of its neighbors. Turkmenistan has signed a delimitation agreement only with Kazakhstan. In light of the delimitations that had taken place, Iran argued that if the states would not agree to the "condominium principle" for joint ownership of the Caspian waters and seabed, then in the case of national delimitation, each state should receive 20 percent of the Caspian's territory.

In July 2001, Iran attempted to stop the process of bilateral delimitation between the Caspian littoral states and the establishment of U.S.-supported east-west export routes. Iranian military gunboats chased vessels commissioned by Azerbaijan that were surveying a southern part of the Caspian that was disputed between Azerbaijan and Iran. The harassment of the survey vessels was accompanied by a large number of Iranian overflights violating Azerbaijani airspace. To deter Iran from further action, Turkey sent a massive air contingent above Azerbaijan's skies, which also restored public confidence and sense of security in Azerbaijan. Turkey and Azerbaijan consider each other allies and enjoy extensive security and military cooperation.

Another Caspian border that is potentially contentious is that between Azerbaijan and Turkmenistan. What Azerbaijan calls the Kyapaz field and Turkmenistan the Serdar field is intensely contested by the two countries, and the lack of concord has left this potentially rich oil field underdeveloped.

Legal issues and potential environmental impacts have also been used by Russia to block the establishment of a natural gas pipeline across the Caspian Sea. The United States has strongly advocated the building of a Trans-Caspian pipeline (TCP) to transport Central Asian gas—primarily from Turkmenistan and Kazakhstan—to Azerbaijan, and to join the South Caucasus pipeline (Baku-Tbilisi-Erzerum), which supplies gas from Azerbaijan to Turkey. Together with the volumes from Central Asia, this pipeline could become an attractive additional source of gas for Europe. Russia adamantly opposes this policy and has taken steps to block it, such as raising the issue of the legal status of the Caspian Sea and calling into question the environmental impact of the pipeline that would cross the Caspian seabed. Moscow's opposition is primarily motivated by the desire to block any significant additional sources of gas to Europe that could offset Moscow's dominance in that market, to leave the Central Asian volumes available as a cheap source of gas for Gazprom to reexport at higher prices, and to retain the dependence of the landlocked Central Asian states on Moscow.

The United States and China: Collision or Coalition?

With the dramatic rise in China's oil consumption beginning in the late 1990s, the subsequent activism of its state-owned oil companies in a variety of oil production and export projects around the globe,[45] and the sustained tightness of the world oil market, many policy-makers and academics are claiming that China and the United States are on a collision course over access to dwindling energy resources.[46] Additional claims include that China will use force against U.S. allies and others in the South China Sea to ensure security of the supply lanes in that region. A number of authors have also claimed that the major and growing energy importers in Asia—China, India, and Japan—are on a collision course as they seek to assure access to energy resources.[47] Following this line of argument, China will also be willing to extend diplomatic assistance and sell potentially destabilizing weapons and weapon components—including nonconventional ones—to Middle Eastern oil exporters to guarantee security of supply. In an article in *Foreign Affairs* titled "China's Global Hunt for Energy" the authors claim that the "need for resources is now driving China's foreign policy."[48] Others argue that the drive for control of energy resources will bring the United States and China into conflict in vying for influence in the Middle East, the largest reservoir of proven oil and gas reserves.[49] Flynt Leverett and Jeffrey Bader claim, for example, that "the prospect for competition between China and other states for control over vital energy resources poses particularly critical challenges to U.S. interests in the Middle East."[50] David Zweig and Bi Jianhai believe that "Oil dependence, in particular, has made China an active player in the Middle East." Furthermore, many authors and policy-makers claim that China's ties with a number of rogue oil producers are undermining U.S. policies to curb human right violations, such as in Sudan, or to contain certain states such as Iran and Venezuela. A U.S. Department of Energy report released in 2006 claimed that China's ties with a number of oil producers that Washington considers despotic regimes "runs counter to key strategic goals of

the United States."[51] Amy Myers Jaffe and Kenneth B. Medlock, III, have
argued that

China has demonstrated a willingness to deepen its oil trading relationships with
countries whose ties to the United States are strained, such as Iran, Sudan and
Libya, taking advantage of U.S. sanctions policy and leading to fears that Beijing
will form oil-for-arms, military-client relations under boycott by the United
States. This has put China into a position of geopolitical rivalry with the United
States.[52]

Are China and the United States indeed on a collision course over
control of energy and natural gas resources? Or, alternatively, do they
actually share common interests in the sphere of energy? From the perspective of energy, China and the United States do have a number of
common traits: both are major producers of oil and coal; both consume
coal extensively; they are the world's top two importers of oil, which is
used primarily in the transportation sector in both states. The two countries are also the world's top two emitters of greenhouse gases, and neither has limits imposed on it under the Kyoto Protocol to the UN
Framework Convention on Climate Change.

Proponents of the argument that Washington and China are on a collision course over energy posit the following: in order to gain access to
energy supplies, China will undermine the United States and international coalition policies through support to a number of oil-producing
rogue states; China will challenge U.S. influence and policies in the Middle East; China will use force to guarantee passage in major sea-lanes in
the world in order to import oil; and China will compete with U.S. allies
in Asia—mainly Japan, India, and South Korea—over access to energy
supplies to Asia.

But there is another way to look at the question of energy in the U.S.-
China relationship. Instead of competing goals, in the sphere of energy
the two countries actually share a number of interests, including low and
stable world oil prices, secure world sea-lanes, and a stable and status
quo Middle East.

In analyzing the potential conflict between China and the United
States over access to energy resources, clearly the focus should be on oil,
not on other major energy sources. China and the United States are the
world's number one and number two producers, respectively, of coal,
and both export it, and they do not compete for natural gas pipeline
supplies or LNG shipments. As we discussed earlier, for states to be in
direct conflict over access to oil sources, the prevailing assumption
needs to be that world oil production does not meet world oil demand
and that there is an actual shortage of oil. However, despite alarmists,

the growth in proven world reserves still outpaces the growth in global consumption.

In addition, it would be a very dire situation that would lead either the United States or China to risk major conflict with each other in order to gain access to oil supplies. In the case of China, oil comprises only a quarter of the state's total energy consumption, and most of that is used by the transportation sector. China's usage of energy in the industrial sphere is still dominated by coal, which is domestically produced. In a pinch, China is less vulnerable to supply shortages than states where industry uses oil and which lack domestic energy sources, such as Japan and South Korea.

When it comes to international efforts to address climate change China and the United States share an interest in voluntary approaches to dealing with the threat of climate change and the resulting constraints on patterns of energy use.

Since, as we have seen, China and the United States are both major coal producers and exporters—with China producing close to three-quarters of its electricity from coal, and the United States close to half—the two also share an interest in the development of coal to liquid technologies, and clean coal and carbon-sequestration technologies that will enable them to continue to consume their coal without major ramifications for climate change.

To be sure, a number of features of China's energy security policy are a cause for concern. China does not rely on international oil markets to acquire supplies, but continues to conclude long-term sales arrangements with a number of suppliers. Chinese oil companies also at times enter into deals that do not seem commercially attractive in order to assure equity oil for China.

At the same time, as part of its energy security policy, Beijing is signaling that it does not seek conflict over vital sea-lanes with the United States and its neighbors: it has preferred investments in expensive oil pipeline projects over increased exports by sea.

Beginning in 2002, China's state-owned oil companies became extremely active in oil exploration and production in a variety of locations, especially Africa. Chinese companies acquired stakes in energy production and transport assets in many locations abroad. This activism of Chinese oil companies took place within the framework of a larger government "Going Out" policy that encouraged companies to compete on the global market. This activism, coupled with deals that did not seem commercially attractive, created fears in the United States that China wants to put its flag on a number of oil sources around the world to ensure supplies for itself. Moreover, Washington views China's investments in rogue states, such as Sudan and Myanmar, as threatening U.S.

attempts to isolate and contain these states. The United States has not only taken issue with Chinese companies' investments in what Washington defines as rogue states, but also barred an attempt by the Chinese company Sinopec to acquire the American oil company Unocal, and worked with other Western states to block Chinese companies from becoming a partner in some production projects in Kazakhstan.[53]

The driving force beyond the activities of the Chinese oil companies is not chiefly political. The role of the nominally state-controlled energy companies in the policy process is complicated, and their profit-oriented goals often set the agenda of their activities. As stated in *The Strategic Implications of China's Energy Needs,*

The interests of the companies are not entirely coincident with those of the government. The companies themselves can use their monopoly of expertise and their political influence to justify their commercial interests in overseas investments through arguing that they serve the government's energy security objectives. In general, the domestic and foreign policy interests of the government, which are critical variables in the conceptualization of energy security, are not part of the same calculus as the interests of the oil companies.[54]

In contrast to China's domestic energy market, profit is to be had in unregulated markets abroad. Profit opportunity is higher in these risky locations, often shunned by Western oil companies, where the durable Chinese oil companies are particularly successful. In many cases, the companies themselves lead the charge to a new market abroad and not the government. Moreover, the activities of the Chinese companies still generate modest amounts of equity oil, or barrels that are actually exported to China. Most of the oil produced with the participation of Chinese companies enters the global market pool. In fact, the activity of the Chinese oil companies, instead of taking away from global oil volumes, actually adds to them, since they increase global oil production and consequently contribute to the lowering of world oil prices. Still, the scale of the activity of Chinese oil companies abroad is still quite limited. The IEA predicts that with the current speed of investment, Chinese oil companies will control only 1 to 2 percent of global output by 2020.[55] As for Chinese activities in countries the United States is trying to contain, the response from the Chinese companies is that the United States has driven them to this behavior because it has blocked or attempted to block them from investments in the United States itself or in more Western-oriented states like Kazakhstan.

Another geopolitical concern—that China's thirst for oil will challenge U.S. influence in the Middle East and undermine U.S. policy there, potentially leading to conflict between Washington and Beijing—is also less worrisome than some commentators have argued.

China's oil exports from the Middle East have contributed to China's gaining an interest in stability and preservation of the status quo in the Middle East. In comparison to policy in the 1970s and 1980s, Beijing's Middle East policies reflect an interest in working with the prevailing powers in the region and not attempting to undermine their stability. Concerned with preserving stability in the region and recognizing the potential spillover effect on its own Muslim minorities, China no longer grants support to nonstate "national liberation movements" operating in the Middle East. As Beijing stated in its 2007 energy doctrine document,

The international community should work collaboratively to maintain stability in oil producing and exporting countries, especially those in the Middle East, to ensure the security of international energy transport routes and avoid geopolitical conflicts that affect the world's energy supply.[56]

A number of the works that warn of conflict emerging between China and the United States are related to China's investments and relations with Iran. However, precisely because of Beijing's growing oil exports from Iran and interest in investments in the oil and gas sector in that country, China has an interest in preventing a nuclear Iran, which clearly would lead to wide sanctions on Iran and increased instability in the Persian Gulf region, threatening China's oil imports. Moreover, China's increasing oil imports from the Persian Gulf actually increase its need for cooperation with the United States: China does not have the capability to secure the sea-lanes from the Middle East to China. Moreover, this security function is carried out by U.S. forces. In fact, China is more vulnerable to instability in the Middle East than the United States in terms of impact on oil supplies, since Beijing has no ability to project its power into the region. And Beijing is not investing significant resources to acquire a blue water navy. At this point, it prefers to invest in expensive pipelines instead of attempting to build naval capability to secure its supplies from the Middle East. It has built a pipeline from Kazakhstan to China and seeks pipelines from Russia and other oil producers in Asia, despite the high cost. In the last decade China has also been increasing its oil imports from areas outside the Middle East, such as Russia, Kazakhstan, and Africa, signaling that it does not intend to confront the United States in the Middle East.

China is certainly a growing power both in Asia and globally, and as with any significant change in power relations, this can lead to conflict in the process of adjustment to this rise on both the regional and global levels. The propensity to conflict in response to that rise will be determined by the actions taken by both Beijing and the other major powers. Competition for limited oil supplies, as seen in this analysis, will not be a major factor in the propensity to conflict. Energy can actually be a field of dialogue in which the United States and China share a number of common interests that can help peacefully accommodate China's rise.

Chapter 5
Security

Energy is a strategically vital commodity, and access to energy is a necessary element of a state's security. For many countries, energy security is an integrated element of foreign and national security policies. Energy's importance becomes particularly clear when world energy markets are tight since concerns about energy security tend to rise. NATO, for example, integrated energy security into its mission in 2006 in the wake of a period of extended high oil prices.[1]

Yet popular discussions of energy security are often fuzzy about what the term means. Many people are confused by the concepts of energy security and energy autarchy (or energy independence). Achieving adequate energy security does not demand that a state can provide in the long term all its energy needs domestically. In fact, in integrated world oil and coal markets, domestically produced supplies do not provide economic advantage to consumers over imported supplies, and they thus impair the ability to achieve one of the elements of energy security, affordability. Traditionally, the United States has taken a global approach to energy security, assessing that the arrival of increased volumes of oil to the world market will lower prices and increase the supply security, regardless whether those volumes were intended to reach U.S. shores. Moreover, Washington views its own energy security as interlinked with that of its allies, and thus needs to promote a global approach to achieving it. Despite these factors, the slogan of "energy independence" has become a frequent rallying call by politicians in the United States and other countries, especially during the 2008 U.S. presidential campaign. Moreover, this goal is enshrined in a number of the official policy documents of President George W. Bush's administration on energy security.

Energy security is widely conceived to have three main components: reliability of supply, affordability of supply, and friendliness to the environment. Energy security is achieved through several means: diversification of energy sources and suppliers, stockpiling of fuel, creation of redundant infrastructure, and promotion of flexibility in fuel use.

Still, achieving this goal is far from simple. Most countries' bureaucracies are not set up in a way that helps them to tackle questions of energy security effectively. Such concerns tend to fall within the purview of many government ministries and agencies, leaving it unclear which entity bears primary responsibility for ensuring energy security. For example, while energy security is necessary for the function of any state military, militaries and military doctrines are generally not equipped for dealing with the full range of energy security problems and so the armed forces are not charged with handling this task.

The response in some Western industrialized democracies has been to opt out of this responsibility altogether. In these countries, there is a growing tendency for the state to retreat from owning, managing, or regulating energy infrastructures and acquiring supplies, yielding to market forces to control energy policy. This policy is shortsighted: at a time when the state needs to better provide energy security, it is abandoning a means of doing so. Just as market forces cannot be trusted to ensure national security, they will not achieve energy security, either. The market does not create the redundancies of supply sources and types that are necessary as part of energy security. Democratic publics do not tolerate extended energy supply disruptions, and they expect their governments to maintain idle capacity to prevent this, despite the fact that it defies economic rationality.

Moreover, the ability of states to ensure their energy security is constrained by other concerns. For example, there can also be a trade-off between energy security and taking steps to contain climate change. This is evident, for instance, in policy on the use of coal. Coal is found in a large number of countries, is the lowest-cost source of electricity production, and can be transformed into a number of versatile uses. However, because of its impact on air pollution and large release of climate-altering gases, coal is not environmentally friendly. Thus, coal usage is good for two elements of energy security—security of supply and affordability—but has trade-offs with promoting friendliness to the environment.

Energy security is also intertwined with physical security factors. For example, the world's shipments of oil and LNG rely in large measure on the ability of the U.S. navy to ensure secure passage on the world's oceans, particularly through three narrow straits that are potential chokepoints for energy trade. Energy infrastructure has been frequently targeted by terrorist and insurgent groups as an inexpensive means of asymmetric warfare against more powerful actors. And nuclear energy seems to offer the tantalizing prospect of having energy security dependent on stable countries such as Canada and Australia until one takes into account that the growth of this industry could lead to more nuclear proliferation crises like those with Iran and North Korea.

Energy Security

As stated earlier, energy security includes three components:

- reliability
- affordability
- environmental friendliness

Reliability of supply means that a state has regular, noninterrupted access to energy in the quantity and forms it requires. Affordability means that it has access to energy supplies at a price that can be sustained economically and promotes economic growth. Friendliness to the environment means that the prevailing form of energy provides for environmental sustainability and does not incur high health costs for residents. In recent years, many states view "friendly to the environment" to mean policies that lead to the reduced release of climate-altering gases.

While all three elements are considered essential to energy security, most states promote some elements more than others. For example, the United States gives deference to reliability of supplies. The EU and its component states tend to place priority on affordability and friendliness to the environment, taking bigger risks with supply reliability. China emphasizes reliability of supply more than affordability or friendliness to the environment. India views affordability as applying not just to existing consumers, but to acquiring energy sources that will give its have-nots access to energy. In recent decades, the United States and Europe have been split on energy security policies, with Washington tending to prod Europe to lessen its dependence on Soviet and then Russian supplies.

States achieve energy security through a number of techniques. These include

- diversity of energy sources
- diversity of suppliers
- storage of energy and strategic petroleum reserves
- redundant energy infrastructure
- flexibility to shift fuels

Diversity of sources means an energy consumption mix that is not overly reliant on one or two types of fuel. Diversity of suppliers involves acquiring energy from suppliers in different geographic locations.

Storing reserve fuel supplies has proved to be one of the most effective tools for achieving greater energy security. NATO member-states are obliged to maintain reserves of their major energy sources equal to three months of consumption. Strategic oil reserves have been maintained by the OECD states since the oil crises of the 1970s and have played an important role in enhancing these states' energy security. In 2007, China initiated the establishment of a strategic petroleum reserve, and this should enhance Beijing's sense of energy security.

A number of states and international organizations view establishing and maintaining competitive energy markets as an important tool for enhancing energy security. However, this tool seems to be losing its efficacy—at least on the supply side—as producers reduce their competitive behavior through the transfer of the bulk of their production to state-controlled oil companies and assume that the market will do a better job at assuring supplies and affordability. National oil companies control 75 percent of the world's proven oil reserves. Many of these companies do not operate on a commercial basis, and are obliged to use a significant portion of their revenues to carry out other state functions rather than investing in ensuring continued or increased production. Accordingly, the consolidation of production under state owners hurts global energy security. It also places the deregulated consumer side at a disadvantage in confronting a unified, state-controlled supply side. In addition, national oil companies are in most cases extremely nontransparent entities, rendering knowledge of their volumes and production trends very unreliable.

Traditionally, energy security policies have focused on oil. Indeed, to a significant extent, world market mechanisms have minimized the risk of oil supply disruptions. With the dramatic rise in natural gas use in recent decades, the focus of energy supply policies has broadened to include it. However, the nature of natural gas supplies and the constraints on its transport mean that natural gas is an even more significant energy security challenge than oil.

The International Energy Agency

The International Energy Agency works to promote the energy security of its member states and attempts to play a role in promoting global energy security. The U.S. government, led by secretary of state Henry Kissinger, was the driver behind the efforts to found the IEA in the early 1970s. NATO members formed its original core of states to the extent that when it was founded it was dubbed an "energy NATO." The IEA is affiliated with the OECD, although its memberships do not completely overlap. The organization headquarters are in Paris, where it was founded in 1974 in response to the 1973–74 oil crises. With major oil producers effectively organizing themselves within OPEC, major consumers felt a need to organize themselves in response. In the words of Edward Morse, former U.S. representative to the IEA, the founding member states sought to "blunt the use of the oil weapon."[2]

The IEA declares its goals as promoting the three basic elements of energy security for the citizens of their member states: "reliable, affordable and clean energy." The IEA has two major functions: sharing oil among member states in the case of short-term supply disruptions, and long-terms plans to reduce dependence on OPEC. Among the tools to achieve these goals is the establishment of strategic petroleum reserves. Most of the IEA member states have also promoted conservation measures in order to decrease consumption. With the exception of the United States and Canada, most IEA member states have used high taxes on gasoline consumption as a measure to reduce consumption. The IEA also performs an essential function by publishing energy statistics that can serve as an alternative to those published by energy companies and governments.

In recent years, the IEA has expanded its mission to promote climate-change prevention policies, market reform, energy technology collaboration, and outreach to nonmember states, especially major energy producers and consumers like China, India, Russia, and the OPEC countries. The IEA conducts energy dialogues with many nonmember states, both major consumers and producers. It has also played a significant role in the work on energy security of the Group of 8 (G-8) forum, which embraces the world's major economies.

Energy Transport Chokepoints

In recent decades, energy trade has become more and more global. Two-thirds of the world's oil trade (crude and refined) is moved by tankers and 25 percent of international natural gas trade is in the form of liquid natural gas. Tankers and LNG vessels generally move along established sea routes. As noted earlier, on these routes there are three main geographic "chokepoints," all of which are narrow straits: the Strait of Hormuz, the Strait of Malacca, and the Bosporus Strait. These straits are critical due to the volumes of oil and LNG that pass through them. Yet, because they are so narrow they could be blocked or access to them could be restricted, which would cause havoc in the international oil market and a tremendous price surge. Aware of the significant impact that blocking one of the straits could have on the world economy, countries such as Iran as well as terrorist organizations are frequently warning that they will target vessels in them.

For instance, in response to international efforts to contain Iran's nuclear program, Iranian leader Ayatollah Ali Khamenei said in a June

2006 speech that if any country attacks Iran, "shipment of energy from this region will be seriously jeopardized." Iran also frequently holds military exercises in which blocking the Strait of Hormuz is part of the scenario, signaling its intent in the event of a conflict.

The Strait of Hormuz is the most critical strait for oil and gas transport, with one-fifth of global energy supply exported through it in 2006. The overwhelming majority of the oil exports of Saudi Arabia, Iran, Iraq, Kuwait, Qatar, and the UAE pass through this body of water, which provides the only sea outlet for the Persian Gulf. At its narrowest point, the Strait of Hormuz is only 34 miles (55 kilometers) wide.

Lawrence Eagles, head of oil markets at the IEA, warns that blockage of the Strait of Hormuz "is probably the biggest single energy-security risk that exists in the world."[3] Keenly aware of their vulnerability, the Persian Gulf oil and LNG exporters have built a number of Hormuz bypass pipelines and are considering additional ones. Many of these pipelines are not operating at full capacity due to the higher costs of pipeline transport versus shipping by sea, but in a time of crisis some of them could be utilized. For instance, a pipeline from Saudi Arabia to the Red Sea has a capacity of 5 million barrels a day, but operated in 2006 at half that level. The UAE has announced plans to build a Hormuz bypass pipeline from Abu Dhabi, with a planned capacity of 1.5 million barrels a day. A number of bypass pipelines run from Iraq to Turkey and Syria, of which only the pipeline to Ceyhan, on the Turkish Mediterranean, is operational. Others, however, could be revived, thus increasing the bypass capacity.

The Strait of Malacca is another critical passage for world oil and LNG trade. Half of the world's oil trade passes through it, including almost all the Middle East oil supplied to Japan and China. The strait links the Indian and Pacific Oceans and is the shortest sea route between the Persian Gulf and Asian markets. At its narrowest point, the strait is only 1.5 miles (2.4 kilometers) wide. This natural bottleneck increases potential for accidents, and renders the vessels there more vulnerable to piracy and potentially to terrorism. If the strait were closed, the extra sailing days would not only add tremendous costs to the shipping of oil, but would cause a further strain on the world's already insufficient tanker capacity. Malaysia has announced that it intends to build a Malacca bypass oil pipeline to alleviate the vulnerability of shipping in the strait.

Still, today the vessels in the Strait of Malacca are the most frequent targets of piracy in the world. These crime networks could also easily be used for terrorist activity. Law enforcement officials in the region frequently mention the possibility that terrorists could use a small vessel filled with explosives to damage or destroy an oil tanker. To ward off such possibilities, Indonesia, Singapore, and Malaysia conduct joint patrols in the strait.

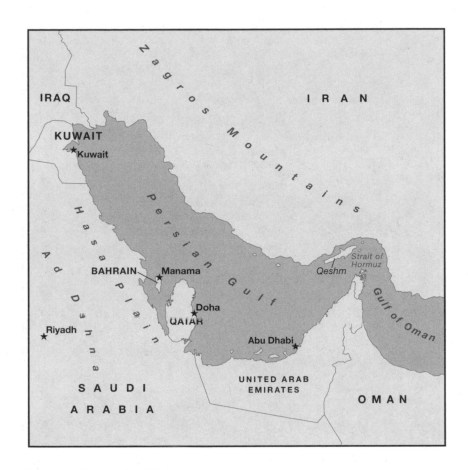

Figure 6. The Strait of Hormuz area.

Figure 7. The Malacca Strait area.

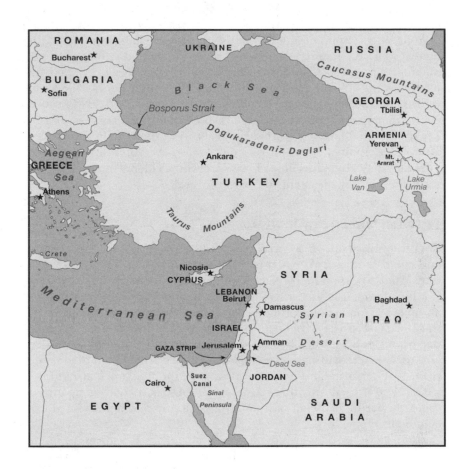

Figure 8. The Bosporus area.

The Bosporus Strait lies in Turkey between Europe and Asia and connects the Black Sea to the Mediterranean Sea. The Bosporus is a critical sea artery for both oil and nonoil trade and is one of the busiest in the world: more than 50,000 vessels pass through it annually, including thousands of oil tankers. The strait is especially crucial for Russian exports, since only Russia's Black Sea ports are operational year-round. The Black Sea is the main route for Russian and the bulk of Kazakhstani oil exports.

At its narrowest point, the Bosporus Strait is only half a mile (0.8 kilometer) wide. It contains a number of sharp curves and strong currents, making ships there especially prone to accidents. Because the city of Istanbul with a population of more than 10 million people flanks its shores, such accidents are particularly threatening. The 1936 Montreux Convention guarantees free passage through the strait. That leaves Turkey with limited leverage to regulate transit in order to improve safety, although a number of major oil companies have voluntarily adopted Turkish safety guidelines in order to prevent accidents and ensure the security of energy shipments through the strait.

Terrorism and Energy Infrastructure

Energy infrastructure has become an attractive target to terrorist groups and combatants in civil strife, providing them with an asymmetric war tool. When world oil markets are tight, attacks on energy infrastructure can fail to impair in any way oil production and transport, yet still have an immense impact on world oil prices. Thus, by targeting energy infrastructure, terrorists can have global impact through very minimal means. An excellent example of this occurred in February 2006, when anti-regime terrorists attacked Saudi Arabia's Abqaiq oil-processing plant. The terrorists did not even make it to the first fence around the facility, and caused only three deaths, but they succeeded in creating a spike of close to $2.50 per barrel in world oil prices, which had a global economic impact.

Middle East terrorist groups also see such attacks as a means of mobilizing popular sentiments against the ruling regimes of Arab oil-producing states. While Osama bin Laden won notoriety for his attacks on the United States, his primary strategic goal has been the demise of Arab oil-producing monarchies, above all Saudi Arabia, which he views as corrupt and anti-Islamic. Bin Laden and his deputies have frequently and explicitly called for their supporters to take actions that will lead to higher world oil prices and have lashed out against selling "cheap oil" to the United States. Bin Laden has termed oil one of the "hinges" of the world economy and a special target of his operations. As early as his 1996 "declaration of war," bin Laden criticized the Middle East oil-producing states for price and production trends that he said were set to suit the American economy. On December 7, 2005, Al Jazeera television aired an Al Qaeda videotape calling on the faithful to attack energy infrastructure because "most of the revenues go to the enemies of Islam, while most of what they leave is seized by the thieves who rule our countries." In addition, following the 2006 attack on the Abqaiq plant in Saudi Arabia, Al Qaeda stated that the attack was part of its "war against the Christians and Jews to stop their pillage of Muslim riches and part of the campaign to chase them out of the Arabian peninsula."[4] Al Qaeda followers have attacked and plotted to attack oil infrastructure a number of times, including an October 2002 attack on a French oil tanker in Yemen and a March 2003 plot to obstruct tanker flow from Morocco.

In any country, energy pipelines and especially their pumping stations, LNG terminals, electricity transmission grids, and power plants represent attractive and, at times, fairly easy targets for terrorists and hackers. The highly computerized automation of much of this infrastructure makes it especially vulnerable. While long-term damage is rarely achieved, the psychological impact of electricity blackouts from saboteurs can be catastrophic. Leon Fuerth, former national security adviser to U.S. vice president Al Gore, has written that

the electric energy system is a particularly strategic and vulnerable part of the U.S. energy infrastructure. . . . The system, if it deserves to be so called, has a well-demonstrated potential for catastrophic failure as the result of natural or accidental human causes. These same weaknesses also make the system an obvious and lucrative target for exploitation by terrorists. It should be noted that physical attack on critical nodes of the system might not be needed if a cyber attack on control systems were attempted and proven to be effective.[5]

Energy infrastructure is a frequent target in the conflict in Iraq and in other venues of civil strife. Between April 2003 and May 2005, 236 attacks took place on Iraqi energy infrastructure. The attacks have contributed significantly to the failure of Iraqi oil production to recover to prewar levels.

Ships carrying LNG have often been presented in the press as "floating bombs" and highly vulnerable to terrorist attack. However, there are different views on the public danger that is truly posed by LNG vessels and facilities. The prevailing view in U.S. government studies is that spills from LNG tankers would create not explosions, but fires with more limited ability to cause damage.[6] Official studies claim that the potential danger is limited since liquefied natural gas cannot be ignited. However, if an LNG spill were to take place it could create a vapor cloud that would be flammable. Intentionally breaching LNG tankers could lead to vapor clouds that would pose a strong danger to people and items within 500 meters (a third of a mile) of the spill, and more limited damage as far as 1,600 meters (a mile) away.[7]

Nuclear Energy and Nuclear Weapons Proliferation

Nuclear energy has become more attractive during periods of rising prices of competing sources of energy due to the extremely low emissions of climate-altering gases its production entails and the industry's improved safety and operating record.[8] Countries such as France and the United States also view nuclear energy as a more secure source of energy than many alternatives, since the largest producers of uranium, its key raw material, are the highly stable democracies of Canada and Australia, and they can provide most of the other elements of a nuclear energy program themselves.

Indeed, nuclear energy boosters like to talk of a "nuclear renaissance," pointing, for example, to the facts that China plans to install 40 gigawatts of nuclear energy by 2020 and that in 2007 U.S. utilities submitted the first license applications to operate a nuclear reactor in thirty years. Yet nonproliferation experts worry that growth in the use of nuclear energy could also lead to proliferation of nuclear weapons. The expansion of nuclear energy programs will increase the amount of fissile material that could be diverted to military or terrorist programs, along with knowledge and trained individuals for nuclear weapons programs. There is a particular concern about fuel-making technologies that enrich uranium or reuse plutonium in spent nuclear fuel as a fuel source. As stated in a Council of Foreign Relations report, "Nuclear Energy: Balancing Risks and Benefits," "fuel-making technologies are dual use: either for creating fuel for peaceful reactors or for producing explosive material for nuclear weapons. Thus, a commercial fuel-making facility represents a latent nuclear bomb factory."[9] In addition, as stated by the Harvard energy expert John Holdren, expanding the use of nuclear energy has "multiplied the opportunities for terrorists to acquire the wherewithal to make nuclear explosives."[10]

In some ways, the recently heightened interest in nuclear energy is nothing new. It tends to occur during times of tight oil market conditions—and now—the associated rise in natural gas prices. For example, similar growth in nuclear energy occurred after the 1970s oil crisis. That growth foundered in the 1980s with the accidents at Three Mile Island (1979) and Chernobyl (1986) and as oil prices plummeted.

Moreover, currently nuclear energy can only play a limited role in addressing energy security concerns. At this time, nuclear energy is used to produce electricity, so except for electricity-fueled vehicles it cannot replace oil in the transportation sector, which accounts for close to 60 percent of world consumption of oil. To be sure, the United States is engaged in a program seeking to use nuclear reactors in producing hydrogen as a potential transportation fuel, but this a long-term research effort with highly uncertain results.

Even as a means of producing electricity, nuclear energy plays at best a tertiary role, accounting for only 16 percent of the world's electricity production. By contrast, coal is used to generate 39 percent of the world's electricity, natural gas 25 percent, oil 25 percent, and hydroelectric power 19 percent. In addition, nuclear energy plants are found in a limited number of states. In 2007 there were 435 nuclear power reactors in 30 countries; a third of the plants are in the United States (103), France (59), and Japan (55).[11]

The growth of nuclear energy has been impeded by four major factors: price, safety, difficulties in disposing of nuclear waste, and weapons proliferation concerns. The main impediment to the growth of use of nuclear energy is its price—it is more expensive than the sources of electricity in widespread use: coal, natural gas, oil. Consequently, in periods of low oil prices, and often subsequent low natural gas prices, interest in nuclear energy wanes. Nuclear energy production has also been constrained due to safety and environmental concerns, in particular, the inability of countries to dispose of the vast amounts of spent fuel, growing by 10,000 metric tons worldwide per year. Furthermore, the potential expansion of nuclear energy has raised concerns about the possibility that materials and technology could be diverted from peaceful use to nuclear weapons or that countries could accumulate sufficient expertise to operate clandestine facilities. Such concerns have been heightened by Iran's pursuit of a clandestine but allegedly peaceful nuclear energy program. That effort has been judged a violation of Iran's safeguards agreement with the International Atomic Energy Agency (IAEA), worth sanction from the UN Security Council, and a potentially dangerous precedent for other nuclear aspirants.

To address such concerns, the IAEA and the United States are promoting policies that seek to restrict uranium enrichment and spent fuel reprocessing—the most proliferation-vulnerable links in the nuclear energy process—to a few locations (primarily existing sites). Although they differ on whether such facilities should be under national or multinational control, the United States and the IAEA agree that if such formulas are not accepted, the global increase of such fuel-making facilities could spur nuclear weapons proliferation. First, such facilities are inherently difficult if not impossible for the IAEA to safeguard effectively against diversion. Second, an increase in the number of states where nuclear reactors are operating, or in the number of safeguarded reactors in some countries such as India, will further stretch already over-taxed IAEA inspectors and budgets, as IAEA director general Mohamed El Baradei has made clear. Third, once a country gains the expertise to operate such a facility, it can build additional secret facilities to produce weapons material. Uranium-enrichment facilities, in particular, can be hidden and are almost impossible to detect without onsite inspections, to which countries are not necessarily required to submit. In addition, the more fissile material in transit or in use, the greater the opportunity for diversion to military programs or theft by terrorists for their own nuclear weapons programs.[12] And nuclear reactors themselves could become objects of terrorist attacks.

Chapter 6
Climate Change

Energy and environmental policies are interconnected: how a state uses energy is one of the most significant factors affecting its environment. At the same time, environmental policies affect energy consumption patterns and prices. The interconnection between energy and environment is most acute in the sphere of climate change: addressing the issue of climate change implies dramatic shifts in energy consumption patterns on a global scale. In addition, climate change policies affect the preferences for which fuels are consumed and thus affect the prices for different energy sources.

A number of the consequences of massive use of fossil fuels—air pollution, dependence on Middle East oil, funding to nondemocratic regimes—have raised questions about the wisdom of the world's continuing dependence on fossil fuels. Until now, due to their relatively low costs and the easy portability of oil and coal, and the diversity of uses of these fuel sources, no major action has been taken to wean the industrialized world from dependence on fossil fuels. However, the threat of climate change and the anticipated costs of adjustment may be significant enough to serve as a catalyst for reducing the use of such fuels in the long term.

Until recently, climate change was seen as an expendable item on the international agenda, confined primarily to the realm of environmental policy. Now, however, climate change is a major concern of leading international and regional political and economic groupings. Climate change is no longer considered an issue relating only to quality of life and the environment, but also one directly affecting human and global security. For example, climate change has been recognized as an international security threat, with the initiation in 2007 of UN Security Council discussions on the topic. Consequently, due to their link to climate change, energy consumption patterns and policies have become an international security issue. As stated by UN secretary general Ban Ki-moon, "Projected changes in the earth's climate are thus not only an environmental concern . . . issues of energy and climate change can have implications for peace and security."[1]

While global public awareness has grown on the need to address climate change, the full international community has yet to agree on a policy mechanism to address the challenge. The lack of coordinated international policy, despite the wide recognition of the dangers of climate change, illustrates the difficulties in the international system of collective action on an issue of such magnitude.[2] Climate change is also a particularly difficult global challenge since it requires current generations to make material sacrifices in order to avert danger to future generations. Moreover, climate change creates a special challenge, since each state is vulnerable to the effects of climate change, but the solution can only be reached globally.

The political debates over how to address the threat of climate changes reflect a number of the larger debates in the international system, such as the responsibility of industrialized countries toward developing countries, the obligations of current populations toward the security and livelihood of future generations, and questions of how to accommodate changes in power relations in the international system, such as the rise of China. While all states are affected by the consequences of climate change, some states will be affected more than others, especially in early changes of the shift. Also, there is no connection between the damage that will be incurred by a state and its level of emissions. Thus, some states will have to disproportionately bear the consequences of the actions of other states. Moreover, the states most immediately threatened by climate change, such as island nations, are among the smallest contributors to the problem.

Climate Change: Background

A wide range of scientists believe that climate change is facilitated by excessive accumulation of "greenhouse gases," particularly carbon dioxide, in the earth's atmosphere. The accumulation of these gases, believed to trap a growing proportion of the energy from the sun's rays, is in turn viewed as intricately linked to consumption of fossil fuels, which release significant amounts of carbon dioxide.

Climate change is a more appropriate term to refer to the consequences of additional "greenhouse gases" in the earth's atmosphere than "global warming." This is because climate change means a broader set of consequences beyond rising temperatures in certain areas. These arc expected to include lower temperatures in other areas, as well as major changes in precipitation and other weather patterns, causing increases in floods and droughts and catastrophic events, such as hurricanes and typhoons.

While certain amounts of climate change are a naturally occurring phenomenon, in recent years a wide consensus has developed among scientists that the current and significant change developing in climate change is induced by human activity, especially its massive use of fossil fuels. Of the fossil fuels, coal use produces the largest amount of carbon dioxide. In comparison to oil and coal, natural gas consumption releases minor amounts of carbon dioxide. Three-fourths of the world's carbon dioxide emissions are produced by burning fossil fuels. The remaining quarter is produced by deforestation and burning of vegetation, which contains large amounts of carbon, as does surrounding soil.

For several decades, oil companies and related lobbies and politicians have battled climate change policy by attempting to sow public doubt about scientific claims that climate change is induced through human activity, especially the use of fossil fuels. The lobbying had been successful until recently in preventing Washington from taking significant action to address climate change. However, in 2005, a shift emerged in the U.S. and global political climate on the issue, leading to substantially increased public demand for policy action. It seems that a major motivating factor for a shift in state policies can be the actions of nature itself. Intensity and frequency of weather-induced natural disasters, minuscule snowfall in Europe, heat waves in Europe, and simultaneous flooding and droughts in China's provinces brought the issue of climate change close to home for citizens across the world, creating public demand for politicians to take action. Moreover, the intensive damage to New Orleans from Hurricane Katrina in 2005 contributed to the crystalliza tion in the United States of public perceptions as to the danger of climate change.

The emergence of a broad scientific consensus also helped convince governments that climate change was a danger and was induced by human activity. In 2007 the UN Committee on Climate Change published its scientific report, which declared that climate change was "unequivocally taking place" and at a high level of certainty and that it was caused by human activity.[3]

Nonetheless, global climate change poses a unique political task, since both its dangers and its solutions are global and require international cooperation. No state can isolate itself from the dangers of climate change. Thus, it creates a unique policy challenge, since a country's own security and economic prosperity becomes dependent on the actions of other states.

In the debates over responsibility for climate change, the major disagreement is over the basic measure for acceptable greenhouse gas emissions: population size or GNP. States with large populations such as China and India claim they should be considered low emitters of greenhouse gases on a per capita basis. Many in the United States claim that since energy consumption rates are a reflection of GNP activity, emissions should be calculated on the basis of a state's GNP.

Climate Change Policies Milestones

The first major convention to address climate change was the UN Framework Convention on Climate Change (UNFCCC), adopted in 1992 at the "Earth Summit" in Rio. The convention has almost universal membership, including the United States. The UNFCCC stated that its objective was to avert "dangerous anthropogenic interference in the climate system" and establish mechanisms for monitoring and analyzing data on emissions of greenhouse gases. But it did not put in place concrete government commitments for limiting emissions.

The subsequent 1997 Kyoto Protocol to the UNFCCC was designed to establish concrete government commitments to limit actions that interfere with the world's climate system. Under the protocol, thirty-eight industrialized nations agreed to cut emissions of six greenhouse gases to an average of 5.2 percent below 1990 levels by 2008–12. In the United States, the Clinton administration signed the Protocol, but did not submit it to the Senate for ratification. The U.S. was thus one of the few countries that did not join. A major feature of the Kyoto Protocol is that it applies fully to industrial countries, but only partially to economies in transition. Developing countries like China and India are not obliged to reduce greenhouse gas emissions, despite the fact that the largest increases in energy use and emissions come from these countries. China and other developing countries claim that the climate change danger was created by decades of emissions from the major developed states whose access to low-cost energy enabled them to acquire their current level of wealth. Thus, according to China, the main burden of addressing climate change should fall on industrialized countries.

The Kyoto Protocol sought to use market mechanisms to reduce greenhouse gas emissions by a system of emissions trading, what is called "cap and trade." This trading mechanism drew on the successful U.S. experience with an emissions-trading program for sulfur dioxide, the key element producing acid rain. The protocol envisioned three forms of trading: (1) purchase of emissions credits abroad, instead of making reductions at home; (2) joint implementation, by which industrialized nations could earn credits when they jointly implement specific project that reduce emissions; and (3) as part of the Protocol's Clean Development Mechanism, industrial countries could receive emissions credits by investing in emissions reduction projects in developing countries. The protocol also allows for states to be credited for "sinks" that remove CO_2 from the atmosphere, through measures such as planting forests.

The Kyoto Protocol has failed to generate significant global action. It was dealt a major blow in March 2001 when U.S. president George W. Bush, soon after taking office, declared that the United States did not intend to become a party to the protocol. Moreover, the Bush administration at that time failed to offer an alternative framework, and thus was perceived globally as not supporting efforts to reverse climate change.

In contrast to the United States, Europe began in 2005 using the treaty's cap and trade system. But it has proved largely ineffective in reducing emissions in Europe. German energy expert Friedemann Müller writes:

Since the signing of the Kyoto Protocol, emissions in the European Union have not changed at a percentage rate significantly different from that of the United States, which is not bound by the Protocol. Taking into account the higher rate of economic and population growth in the United States, the question must be answered, how empirically founded the argument is that the path taken by the Europeans will lead to the desired goal.[4]

In retrospect, the Kyoto Protocol looks like a rushed political effort by the governments of a number of industrialized states to show their publics that they were taking action on climate change. Since its approval a number of flaws have become evident.

First and foremost, the protocol places no obligations on developing countries to cut their emissions. Indeed, in 2007 China overtook the United States as the world's largest emitter of greenhouse gases. Furthermore, China's emissions rate and those of other developing countries is expected to grow. In addition, the protocol creates opportunities for leakage of emissions, which means that industrialized countries can shift their production to states that do not have emissions limits. This mechanism leads to no improvement in climate change and also to loss of revenue for industrialized states.

Critics also claim that the 1990 date for emissions rollback levels was chosen arbitrarily and favors some states and disfavors others. The biggest benefactors of the 1990 level are Russia and other former Soviet republics, which experienced a large drop in industrial output following the Soviet breakup. If the Kyoto system of emissions trading were to be adopted universally, Russia, Ukraine, and other former Soviet republics that experienced industrial collapse after 1990 could earn billions of dollars by selling emissions credits to industrialized states, without changing their actual level of emissions. Russia might possess carbon credits worth over $50 billion. As stated by a spokesman for a Gazprom subsidiary company, "Russia is the Saudi Arabia of carbon."[5] Another flaw in the Kyoto system is that there is neither an accurate measure nor adequate authority to evaluate the emissions impact of different activities—either emissions reduction efforts or "sink" projects aimed to absorb CO_2, such as forestation. More broadly, the emissions cap-and-trade program that was the main feature of Kyoto, while successfully implemented in the United States, had never been tried elsewhere, let alone on a global scale. Based on the experience of other handouts to the developing world, there is no basis to assume that developing countries that would receive free equipment to reduce their emissions, allowing industrialized countries to continue to emit, would make the effort or pay for the resources to maintain and operate the equipment.[6]

In addition, in contrast to the domestic legal setting, international law does not provide a strong framework for security of property rights.[7] Thus, unlike the sulfur dioxide emissions trading program in the United States, a global trade in credits is not backed by an effective legal or enforcement framework. In addition, like many other international regimes, the protocol provides few penalties for violators or defectors from the treaty, which means that there is little penalty for those who decide to abort their commitments. Defection of a couple of key players could undermine the entire system.[8] Moreover, a Kyoto-type trading system requires accurate reporting and transparency on emissions. This is technically very difficult and highly unlikely to be realized due to the economic costs and benefits of reported actions.

The Kyoto Protocol framework will expire in 2012, and a series of international conferences have been convened to navigate a new international framework for contending with climate change. The first of these conferences was held in Bali, Indonesia, in December 2007. At the Bali conference, a road map document was adopted as a framework for continuing diplomacy over a new treaty, but no fundamentally new framework or binding emissions reductions were adopted. The road map was endorsed unanimously, including by the U.S., EU, China, and India. A conference was held in Poznan, Poland in December 2008, and one is slated for December 2009 in Copenhagen, Denmark, which aims to complete the adoption process of a framework to replace the Kyoto Protocol.

Anticipated Next Steps

The core of the world's leading scientists, a number of governments of major powers, and wide segments of the world's populations recognize climate change as a global threat that can have a major effect on economies around the world, the safety and health of wide groups of the world's people, and the habitability of the earth for humans and other species. Despite this wide recognition and public demand for action, few concrete, effective steps have been taken. The Kyoto Protocol itself did not succeed in making a dent in climate change. John Holdren, a Harvard expert on climate change policy, claims that even prior to its expiration the Kyoto Protocol has become

irrelevant. The United States has refused to ratify it, and most of the countries that did aren't going to meet their targets. Plus, there has never been any agreement on what the penalty is for not meeting those targets. The key questions now are what the world collectively is going to do for an "encore" at the end of the Kyoto commitment period in 2012, and what the major emitting countries— including especially the United States and China—are going to do individually in the meantime.[9]

Previous conventions on averting climate change attempted to achieve wide consensus and participation of the worlds' states. The next stage of policy most likely will focus on cooperation between a core group of the world's powers and the chief emitters.[10] Toward the end of the Bush administration, it seemed that Washington focused on achieving consensus and cooperation among the top emitters—especially China—instead of wide agreement encompassing most of the world's states. The Bush administration also preferred a voluntary commitment to reduce emissions, instead of a binding convention.

The United States and China have each signaled that they would be willing to take significant action to avert climate change if the other adopted similar measures. The G-8, especially under the leadership of German chancellor Angela Merkel, has declared its readiness to take serious steps to avert climate change. An expanded G-8 plus two (China and India) that would encompass the bulk of the emissions of greenhouse gases could be an effective forum to tackle the task. This framework may be especially attractive for India and China, since it provides them an opportunity to expand cooperation with the G-8 framework.

Many states, in attempting to enhance their energy security, may be exacerbating climate change. In attempting to cope with the world's tight oil market, replacement of oil and gas with synthetic liquids and gases made from tar sands, oil shales, and coal has become increasingly attractive. However, these energy forms release more carbon dioxide than their conventional counterparts. Likewise, tearing down forests and raising wetlands to make way for more biofuel crops is counterproductive, since deforestation and burning of vegetation release vast amount of carbon and denies the absorption of carbon by these vegetations.

Climate Politics and Ethics

Policy options for dealing with climate change raise a number of ethical and practical questions. As with security of supply, market forces, left undisturbed, will not avert climate change. It is difficult to think of a business that would significantly scale back profit to ensure that future owners of a factory will be able to prosper. This is a core problem of climate change policy. It requires current populations to make material sacrifices to avert danger to future generations. Consequently, many industrialized states may have to rethink how much the state should retreat from the energy market. It may have to retain a large role, at least in the form of carbon taxes or major regulation, to address climate change.

Beyond the physical and economic threats from climate change, policies to avert it raise a number of ethical questions. The cap-and-trade mechanism in the Kyoto Protocol offered legitimacy to the ethically questionable practice of paying to continue to release greenhouse gases. Within the framework of the Protocol, the practice becomes more questionable, since the emissions can be passed to states like Russia and the Ukraine, which, as we have seen, experienced dramatic drops in emissions in the post-Soviet downturn. Thus, emissions trade within the Protocol framework could lead to a situation in which emissions were contained within the legal limits but did not actually change.

Furthermore, the businesses that have sprung up to provide individuals with an opportunity to offset carbon use also raise moral questions. Harvard political philosopher Michael Sandel argues that the danger "is that carbon offsets will become, at least for some, a painless mechanism to buy our way out of the more fundamental changes in habits, attitudes and way of life that are actually required to address the climate problem."[11] In addition, there is no process to follow up and monitor that projects are actually established and maintained or that they truly reduce or absorb the carbon emissions. On the wider ethnical question, Thomas Friedman put a nice comical twist on the topic: he suggested that business should be set up to offset any of the violations of the Ten Commandments, such as adultery and murder, not just carbon emissions.[12]

In terms of the distribution of responsibility between states, developing countries claim that they are not responsible for most of the greenhouse gases trapped in the earth's atmosphere today and thus the industrialized countries that created the problem should have to make the material and other sacrifices to solve it. In addition, spokesmen for the developing countries clam that they should have the right to benefit economically from use of low-cost fossil fuels, since these contributed significantly to the economic position of the United States and Europe today. By contrast, industrialized nations claim that no dent in greenhouse gases can be made without the participation of the developing countries that are today the top emitters. Moreover, they say states like China and India should benefit from the efficiency technologies that have been developed recently so as not to not make the same mistakes as the industrialized states that were not aware of the danger of climate change.

Addressing climate change creates a significant challenge to the sovereignty of the state in the international system. State sovereignty is one of the fundamental principles of the current international political system. However, if significant climate change occurs, no state can protect itself from its impact, and thus state security can become dependent on the actions of other states. In addition, addressing global climate change requires states to radically change the organization of their economies and lifestyles for the sake of a common global goal. While states have combined action in order to address other common environmental threats, such as depletion of the earth's ozone layer, no environmental threat to date has demanded such a radical change in state behavior, nor has it presented such a potential catastrophic threat to the livelihood of people, if it is not addressed.

Chapter 7
Russia

Russia is the world's largest energy exporter and the second-largest energy producer. Already the largest exporter of natural gas, Russia also holds the world's largest natural gas reserves, second-largest coal reserves, and eighth-largest proven oil reserves, with the potential for considerable further growth in the oil and gas sectors since wide swaths of Russian territory remain uncharted. Russia is also a major producer of nuclear energy and aims to increase its exports of reactors and technology, as well as expand fuel and waste processing and storage.[1] Revenues from energy export are Russia's largest source of foreign earnings and have played a significant role in its economic development since the last quarter of the nineteenth century. Energy export policies are an integral element of Russia's overall foreign policy. The energy sector plays an important role in domestic politics in Russia, and also affects the country's foreign policy.

At the same time, Russia has a far more diversified economy than most of the world's major energy producers, especially the Persian Gulf states. Approximately 20 to 25 percent of Russia's GDP is derived from oil and gas, and revenues from this sector provide not quite 37 percent of the state budget.[2]

Geography plays a central role in Russia's energy export opportunities and policies. Russia borders on two of the world's major energy import markets: the European Union and China, making it an obvious supplier of natural gas and oil to both. At the same time, Russia's geography serves as a potential constraint on its freedom of export. Russia is in a sense a landlocked state: most of its ports are not operational year-round due to weather conditions. Its most accessible port, Novorossiysk on the Black Sea, is closed to tankers many days of the year due to weather conditions and also requires transit through the congested Bosporus Strait. Consequently, a major feature of Russia's energy and foreign policies is reducing dependency on routing exports through transit states.

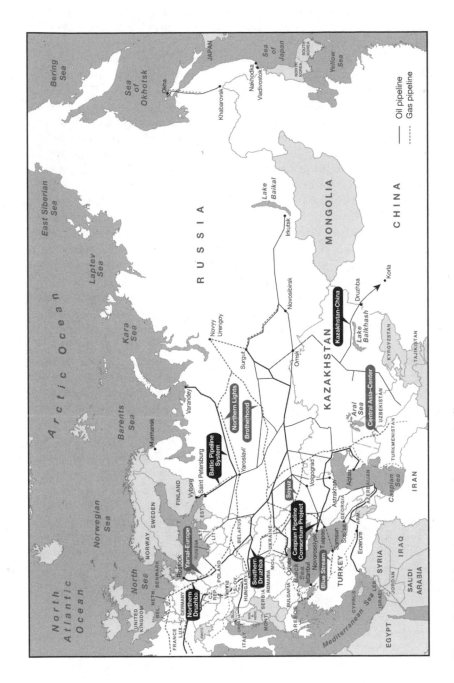

Figure 9. Russia's major ports and export pipelines.

Two key documents for understanding Russia's energy policies are the state energy policy strategy published in 2003 and an academic article written by Vladimir Putin for the journal of the St. Petersburg Mining Institute before he became president of Russia.[3] Both documents demonstrate that Russia views its energy resources as a strategic resource to propel economic development as well as an important geopolitical tool.

While many governments wonder whether Russia can be trusted as a reliable energy supplier, Moscow itself is concerned with the security of its markets and access to them. As the government states in *Energy Strategy of Russia Until 2020*, Russia's "export infrastructure must be sufficiently diversified to allow exports in all directions."[4] With limited sea access for oil export and the need to rely on pipelines to export natural gas, Moscow exports the bulk of its natural gas and a large proportion of its oil through transit states. Moscow's dependence on transit states and its drive to reduce its vulnerability are important factors in its energy export and foreign policies. A number of Russia's transit states are NATO members or states with which it does not have particularly friendly relations, complicating energy export policies. Indeed, the bulk of Russian oil export goes through the Black Sea port of Novorossiysk (and past NATO member Turkey) and through transit states along the Druzhba pipeline to Eastern Europe,[5] both complicated and vulnerable routes. Consequently, a major feature of Russia's energy and foreign policies is attaining leverage over bordering transit states to decrease the risks of its dependence on them. Russia has also taken steps to reduce dependence on risky transit domestically, and has spent significant funds to build bypass pipelines around the rebellious province of Chechnya.

One of the ways Russia promotes its policy of gaining leverage over its transit states is through buying up energy infrastructure in neighboring states. Russia makes it a formal goal to acquire energy infrastructure in the former Soviet republics. It also strives to restore a unified electric grid between the states. At the same time, Moscow does not allow foreign companies to buy energy transit and distribution infrastructure in Russia. Consequently, Moscow has not ratified the European Union Energy Charter, and thus has not allowed European companies reciprocity of full access to Russia's energy market.

One of Russia's major energy goals is retaining its role as the main exporter to the EU gas market. Moscow has gone to great lengths to ensure its predominance in the market, including investing in extremely expensive infrastructure that circumvents transit states, and purchasing routes that could allow potential competitors, such as Turkmenistan and Iran, to enter the European market directly. It seems also that Moscow strives to supply gas to China and other Asian markets. If this should materialize, Moscow would be in a position to play the European and Chinese markets against each other, and achieve much higher prices for its gas supplies.

Russia's energy ownership structure is formally mixed, allowing both state and private ownership; it also allows both Russian and foreign ownership of energy production and some types of infrastructure. However, the Putin administration created tremendous obstacles to both private and foreign producers. Moreover, oil export from Russia is controlled by the state-controlled pipeline company Transneft. In the natural gas arena, the state-controlled company Gazprom dominates production and controls distribution and export. Consequently, although Russia strives for membership in the World Trade Organization (WTO), it has negotiated exceptions for the energy sector and has not sought to liberalize this sphere.

Currently, the majority of Russia's natural gas and oil is produced in western Siberia. Eastern Siberia remains largely unexplored. It may contain enormous oil and natural gas riches, but transport of these resources over vast distances to markets will demand extensive investment. Russia is still weighing whether the benefits justify these costs.

This chapter will examine the role oil and gas have played in Russian history, energy consumption patterns and export trends, and current politics and policies. It will focus on the question of Moscow's energy-export policies and their role in Russia's foreign relations.

Oil and Gas in Russia's History

Since the industrial age, Russia has been a central player in the world oil market. At the turn of the twentieth century, czarist Russia was the world's largest oil exporter. During this period, Baku (now capital of the independent country of Azerbaijan) was part of the Russian empire and the world's largest crude oil producer. An oil boomtown, Baku attracted capital from around the globe, including the Rothschild and Nobel families. During World War II, one of Hitler's strategic targets was to capture the Baku oil fields. By the 1970s, those fields had languished, but the Soviet Union still surpassed the United States as the world's largest producer of petroleum and at times, the world's largest oil exporter. In 1993 Russia became the world's largest natural gas exporter.

Through much of the post-World War II period, the Soviet Union was the major supplier of oil and gas to its Warsaw Pact allies in Eastern Europe. Oil was provided to its Eastern European client states mainly through the Druzhba pipeline, which functioned in this period on a barter basis, with the Soviet Union receiving payment in the form of machinery and other manufactured goods instead of hard currency.[6]

This system was economically disadvantageous to the Soviet Union, which could have sold the oil on world markets and purchased more technologically advanced goods with the hard currency revenues.

During the 1970s, Russia became a major energy exporter to Western Europe and world markets as well. These sales became the Soviet Union's major source of foreign currency; oil sales to world markets averaged a million barrels a day. Extensive natural gas exports also began to Western Europe. The first major Soviet natural gas pipeline to Western Europe was built in 1973 to Germany.

Despite its vast resources and major export role, Soviet oil production began to decline during the 1970s. In addition, inefficient domestic use of energy led to assessments that consumption would rise in the Soviet Union. These trends led the U.S. Central Intelligence Agency (CIA) to publish an infamous report estimating that the Soviet Union would become a petroleum importer by the mid-1980s, and warning that Moscow would become a competitor to the United States for access to such supplies, especially in the Middle East.[7]

Due to declining oil production in the Soviet Union and the dramatic fall in world oil prices in the 1980s, the Soviet Union in this period lost a significant source of revenue. Some have cited the loss of revenues from energy exports as an important factor that spurred the reform process in the Soviet Union and even contributed to its collapse in 1991.

Oil and gas production was further weakened by the disruption of the reform period itself and the turmoil connected with the fall of the Soviet Union. The ensuing erratic process of privatizing Russia's oil resources led to a further severe reduction in Russia's oil during the early 1990s as most of Russia's oil fields and some of its natural gas resources fell into private ownership. Vladimir Putin, former Russian president, described this time as when "the state let strategic management of the natural resource complex slip from its hands."[8]

During this period, foreign investment in Russia's oil and gas sector was also encouraged, and many of the world's major energy companies invested in exploration, production, or export projects in Russia. For instance, the largest foreign investment project in Russia in the initial post-Soviet period was the Caspian Pipeline Consortium (CPC) project, which built a major oil pipeline through Russian territory to the Russian port at Novorossiysk for the export of Kazakhstani oil. The project received billions of dollars in investments from U.S. companies, led by Exxon, Mobil, and Chevron, and enjoyed strong U.S. government support.

However, the majority of Russia's oil and gas assets were acquired in the 1990s by a small group of Russian citizens often referred to as oligarchs. While some Russian citizens acquired control of the state's energy riches during the tenure of Russian president Boris Yeltsin in the 1990s in a legal manner, most of them gained the resources through inside connections with Russian government officials or by manipulating the multiple owners of small numbers of ownership shares distributed to the employees of idle facilities. One of the major schemes was the "loans for shares" program. Under this program privately owned Russian banks made cash loans to the Russian government and received in return payment in ownership of oil and natural gas resources. Often government officials cooperated in ensuring that the government would default on the loans so the lenders could then acquire their desired properties at bargain prices.[9] Many of the private companies succeeded in rapidly increasing Russia's energy production and many became active in commercial investment abroad. One of the most successful in this period was the now defunct Yukos Company.

When Putin came to power as president in 1999, the majority of Russia's oil production was in private hands. Putin's administration dramatically changed the government's previous laissez-faire policy toward the private energy companies and foreign ownership and investment in the Russian energy sector. Initially, the government significantly raised taxes on oil exports in order to capture a greater proportion of the oil profits. Following this, a number of owners of major energy resources in Russia surrendered their energy properties and went into exile. In the most extreme and publicized case, Putin launched a campaign in 2003 against the president of Yukos, Mikhail Khodorkovsky, who was jailed for tax evasion. The company's assets were sold off and the sale was manipulated in order to allow the state-controlled company Rosneft to gain a controlling interest. Scholars still disagree as to the motivation for Putin's assault on Khodorkovsky and Yukos, with most citing Khodorkovsky's potential political ambitions, which challenged Putin's grip on Russia. Khodorkovsky also challenged Transneft's monopoly on oil export infrastructure by attempting to build independent pipelines to China and through Russia's Arctic port of Murmansk. Either way, the demise of Yukos, one of the most efficient companies in Russia, hurt Russia's oil production ability.

By 2005, the Russian state had regained control of a large proportion of Russia's oil and gas sector: 30 percent of oil production and 51 percent ownership of Gazprom, which produces more than 90 percent of the state's natural gas. In addition, the Kremlin had retained full control of the state's oil pipeline transport system.[10] In 2007, Russia further pushed out foreign investors from ownership of gas and oil production projects, using a series of threats to revoke operations' licenses and claiming it acted because of environmental concerns. Among the companies that relinquished properties were BP, which had a stake in the

Kovykta gas field in East Siberia, and Royal Dutch Shell and two Japanese companies, which were coerced into relinquishing a controlling share in oil and gas development on Sakhalin Island off the Pacific Coast. Of course, as soon as Gazprom took over the projects, Russia's Ministry of Natural Resources no longer had any environmental concerns about the project. Russia also created obstacles to the operations of the CPC pipeline that transits Kazakhstani oil through Russian territory as a means to tighten its control over Kazakhstan, including deterring it from joining proposed pipeline plans that circumvent Russia, such as the Trans-Caspian pipeline.

In many oil-producing states, revolutions and regime changes often lead to dramatic standstills in production, sometimes taking decades for recovery. Russia was able to recover from the post-revolution mayhem within a decade of the Soviet demise. Revenues from oil exports have been key to Russia's improved economic performance since making that recovery in 1999. In 2005, for example, the oil and gas sector represented 20 percent of the state's GDP, and generated over more than 60 percent of the state's export revenues. Despite the chilling effects of the Yukos affair and other challenges to foreign ownership of energy production in Russia, this sector accounted for a third of the foreign direct investment in Russia in 2007.[11] The heavy dependence on oil and gas exports, however, leaves the Russian economy at risk to the fluctuations of the prices in these commodities.

Russia's Domestic Consumption

Russia's domestic energy consumption picture is unique. More than half its energy consumption is provided by natural gas, and its oil consumption is declining. In 2007, oil was 19 percent of Russia's total energy consumption, down from 27 percent at the time of the Soviet breakup. This contrasts with most other highly industrialized states where coal consumption retains a significant proportion of the overall state energy consumption and oil is more prominent than in Russia's consumption pattern. Compare this with the European Union average, where oil accounts for 43 percent of the energy use and coal close to 15 percent.

Russia's domestic energy market is heavily subsidized and extremely inefficient. Two-thirds of Russian gas consumed in homes is sold at prices barely above production costs. The government has set itself the goal of ending these subsidies and slowly transferring the domestic market to world energy prices. This is intended to free up energy supplies for further export and increase the incentives for higher production. In contrast to the energy export market—controlled by Gazprom—independent natural gas companies are allowed to operate in Russia's domestic market. Since they are all in all more efficient than Gazprom and their production and operating costs are lower, they can make a living out of this regulated, low-price market. If the independents were allowed to continue to work in the domestic market after the end of subsidies, the independent gas producers would have an opportunity to improve their standing.

Currently, nuclear power plants account for 17 percent of Russia's electricity generation. When he was president, Putin declared a target of raising this to at least 25 percent by 2030.

The Role of Russia's Energy Sector in Politics and Policies

Russia's energy sector and the political leadership are intricately intertwined both formally and informally. The election in March 2008 of former Gazprom chairman Dmitri Medvedev to succeed president Vladimir Putin is a sterling example. Formally, senior Kremlin officials sit on the boards of the major state-controlled entities such as Gazprom and Rosneft. In addition, there is a revolving door for officials between the formal political structure and the leadership of the state-controlled companies. During his presidency, Putin maintained that the state must play a large role in regulating the development and use of Russia's energy sector, regardless of the ownership structure.[12] State-controlled enterprises are thus compelled at times to undertake tasks determined by the state or at prices set by the state, often to the chagrin of the private shareholders and company managers.

The most important players in Russia's energy policies and politics are Gazprom, Transneft, and the Unified Energy Systems of Russia (UES). UES has a virtual monopoly on Russia's electricity production and distribution. Gazprom controls almost all Russia's natural gas production and the entire natural gas pipeline network, and is the largest producer of natural gas in the world. Transneft maintains a monopoly over Russia's oil pipeline network. Thus, while local private and foreign companies can explore for and produce oil and natural gas in Russia, these companies are still dependent on the state-controlled infrastructure for the export of oil and gas. Consequently, the independent exporters must maintain good relations with the two companies and with Moscow in order to have access to the export infrastructure. Through this mechanism of retaining control of the export infrastructure, Moscow also retains control over the activities of foreign and other independent oil producers.

Transneft was established in 1992 as the successor to the Soviet-era state entity Glavtransneft. Its limited capacity and excessive bureaucratic obstacles are major constraints on Russian oil exports, with Russian crude exporters encountering regular bottlenecks in oil export capacity. Transneft's capacity problems are evident in the fact that a significant portion of Russian oil is transported via railway, which is considerably more expensive than using pipelines.[13] The only exception to Transneft's monopoly in Russia is the Caspian Pipeline Consortium, which transports oil from Kazakhstan to Novorossiysk. This pipeline transits Russian territory and in theory also could export Russian production.

Gazprom was established in 1989 on the ruins of the Soviet Ministry of Gas Industry. The third-largest company in the world, it supplies approximately a quarter of Europe's natural gas consumption and it is expected to reach close to 50 percent by 2015. The government of Russia owns 51 percent of Gazprom. The rest is held by public shareholders: shares were offered on the Russian stock market beginning in 1996. Gazprom's exports are the largest source of hard currency for Russia and its tax payments account for nearly a fourth of the state's federal tax revenues. Due to its control over the gas transit infrastructure, it can ward off competitors in Russia.

While benefiting from its control over the pipeline system, Gazprom is also burdened with state responsibilities. Critically, the company is obligated by law to provide the gas for the heat and power of Russia's domestic market at government-regulated prices (approximately $28 per thousand cubic meters in 2007).[14] As noted earlier, the domestic price barely covers production costs and is close to a tenth of the price Russia received at the time for natural gas from its European customers. In addition, in order to decrease Russia's dependence on transit states, the government has required that Gazprom pay for the construction of expensive bypass and parallel export pipelines to European markets, consuming a substantial proportion of its revenues.

Gazprom's extensive investments in recent years in gas and power distribution networks in Western Europe may be partly at the Kremlin's behest. Accordingly, the company underinvests in expanding natural gas production in Russia. Many researchers believe that Gazprom will have difficulty meeting its supply commitments to foreign markets if it does not begin to invest more significantly in increasing production.

Russia hopes to develop extensive liquefied natural gas exports. Should LNG production not fall under Gazprom's control, this could provide new export opportunities for alternative producers. However, in light of the 2007 government takeover of LNG development on Sakhalin Island, and the expulsion of foreign companies from these projects, LNG exports do not appear likely to provide a significant challenge to Gazprom's dominance.

Indeed, Gazprom's greatest competition may come from other state-controlled energy enterprises, which often compete between themselves for control of assets. Following Yukos's demise, for example, Gazprom attempted to attain a number of Yukos assets, but found itself in competition with the state-controlled oil company Rosneft. Putin was forced to intervene personally to end the competition between the two conglomerates over Yukos's properties. In addition to its attempts to acquire oil assets, Gazprom succeeded in 2008 in making inroads into Russia's coal resources. In February it attained control of the Siberian Coal and Energy Company through a merger agreement. Through this acquisition, Gazprom plans to increase the use of coal for domestic electricity production to free up more natural gas for export.

Russia's Energy Export Trends

Russia's energy goals are well integrated into its foreign and national security polices. For instance, the government's 2003 energy strategy document states that the "energy factor is a fundamental element within Russian diplomacy." Russia's natural gas and oil export policies contain a number of major goals: maintaining stable high-paying markets for its natural gas; reducing dependence on the transit of energy exports through neighboring states; sustaining dominance as the main natural gas supplier to the European Union; gaining control of neighboring states' transport and distribution systems both for economic gain and to increase political leverage over former Soviet republics; and expanding oil production and Russia's share of the world market. For example, for the first time Russia is considering building export pipelines for oil and natural gas to Asian markets, which also would enhance its bargaining position in supplying gas to Europe.

Moreover, Russia's political leadership sees its energy wealth as an important tool for Moscow to increase its global power. In fact, Putin, who is now prime minister, addressed this question in his doctoral dissertation, "Mineral Natural Resources in the Strategy of Development of the Russian Economy."[15] Putin claims that Russia's energy resources can help the state facilitate the integration process with other states, and that in its natural resource policy Russia must "take a high degree of responsibility in taking various decisions about domestic and foreign economic policy, aimed at furthering the geopolitical interest and maintaining the national security of Russia."[16] Likewise, the 2003 energy strategy states that Russia should secure its political interests in neighboring countries in Europe and Asia through natural gas, and its global interests through oil.

Still, Russia views its immense energy exports as a double-edged sword. On the one hand, oil and gas exports serve as the state's major source of foreign income and investment and the largest source of state income. Moreover, Russia's status as a major oil and gas exporter gives it considerable clout in a variety of regions and helped it crawl back into a powerful position in the international arena following the Soviet collapse. At the same time, energy profits are extremely volatile and leave the Russian economy in a position of long-term instability (Moscow is quite conscious of its economic vulnerability). Furthermore, a number of factors add to the volatility of Russia's energy exports: lack of multiple year-round ports, the vast distances that separate Russia's major natural gas markets from the source of production, and the location of transit states between Russia and the major markets in Europe. As stated in the Introduction, Russia is almost landlocked: most of its natural gas exports and 40 percent of its oil trade pass through transit states. Over a third of Russia's foreign trade takes place with the European Union, and 80 percent of that passes through transit states.[17] As foreign minister Sergei Lavrov has noted, "We depend on Europe for our exports and we also need stable and reliable demand."[18]

Russia views its transit vulnerability not just from an economic perspective, but as a matter of national security. Seymon Vainshtock, chief of Transneft, has stated a number of times that transit is a matter of state strategy and that for Russia "Transit is a sacred cow."[19] Vainshtock declared that Russia should strive to "get rid of transit dependence."[20]

In an attempt to reduce its vulnerability to transit obstructions, Moscow has taken several steps, including commissioning expensive alternative transit infrastructure, subsidizing energy exports to neighboring states in order to attain control over their transit infrastructure, and halting energy supplies as a punitive measure to states that obstruct transit and as means to obtain control over energy infrastructure in neighboring states. In addition, a major feature of Russia's foreign and security policy is retaining the free-passage regime that rules movement in the Bosporus Strait, which has aided cooperation with Turkey and catalyzed the excellent relations that have developed between the two states in the post-Soviet period.

Russia's investment decisions on its transport infrastructure show that Moscow strongly prefers costly investments in constructing new direct export outlets to Europe over servicing and expanding existing facilities through the Baltic states, Ukraine, and Belarus.[21] As Lavrov has said, "We wish to diversity the routes of energy export."[22] Analysis of the transit transport data shows that Russia is prepared to pay a high cost to accomplish this goal. In addition, Russia is willing to expend significant funds for its transport autarky in terms of investments in new transport infrastructures providing a direct sea outlet from its own territory.[23]

Concrete examples of these bypass and parallel projects are the Yamal-Europe natural gas pipeline through Belarus and Poland and on to Germany (built in 2005), and the planned trans-Baltic pipeline that will enable direct supply from Russia to Germany. Prior to the building of the Yamal-Europe pipeline, nearly 80 percent of Russia's gas exports to Europe transited Ukraine. The proposed 745-mile (1,200-kilometer) Baltic seabed project would further decrease Ukraine's leverage, but will cost an estimated $5 billion. Russia has also constructed a new oil terminal in Primorsk on the Gulf of Finland to divert traffic from the Baltic states.[24]

As part of its policy to minimize dependence on the energy transit trade, Gazprom has subsidized natural gas prices and provided oil in return for transit rights through neighboring states. In 2004 Russia began to condition the continued subsidy of exports of oil and gas to neighboring states on their agreement to surrender their transit and domestic distribution infrastructure to Gazprom. Some countries, such as Armenia and Belarus, agreed to this policy and continue to receive subsided natural gas and oil, albeit at a much higher price than they were accustomed to in the 1990s. Countries that did not agree to surrender their domestic energy distribution infrastructure, such as Georgia and Azerbaijan, were forced to pay close to European market level prices for natural gas in 2005 and 2006 respectively. In some cases, Gazprom has acquired control of the supply and transit infrastructure through third companies, including those it has established for just this purpose. For example, as part of the resolution of a winter 2006 crisis with Ukraine, a new Swiss-registered entity, SP RosUkrEnergo, was established to control acquisition of Turkmen gas to the Ukrainian market.

A major feature of Russia's energy export policy is to maintain its predominance in natural gas exports to the European Union as EU use of this relatively environmentally friendly fuel source grows. In 2007, Russia supplied approximately a quarter of the natural gas consumed in the European Union, with an expansion of the Russian share planned. Already, Russian supply accounts for a much larger percentage of natural gas imports in these EU countries: Austria (77 percent), Germany (41 percent), and Poland (69 percent).[25]

Moscow has gone to great lengths to obstruct potential supply competitors from reaching the European market, to preserve its dominance and thus its ability to guarantee high prices, a stable market, and political influence. Two major potential natural gas competitors exist: Iran and the combined supply from Central Asia and Azerbaijan.

Iran is the most formidable potential rival. It sits on the second-largest natural gas reserves in the world, surpassed only by Russia. Iran does not export natural gas in significant quantities, in part because most of its neighbors are themselves natural gas producers or very small markets, and Tehran is in fact a net natural gas importer. In addition, as of 2009, Iran had no LNG facilities.

To block Iran's entry into the European gas market, Gazprom has bought up, often at exorbitant prices, infrastructure that could provide Iran a potential link to European markets. One of the most obvious examples is Gazprom's April 2006 purchase of a natural gas pipeline from Iran to Armenia that opened in March 2007. Armenia is a tiny natural gas import market, but it borders on Georgia, which in turn, borders on markets in southern Europe.

To block the Armenian route for Iranian gas, Gazprom forced Armenia to reduce the pipeline's circumference by almost half from the original design of a major gas export pipeline, preventing significant expansion of the volumes it carries. Armenia's president, Robert Kocharian, also granted Gazprom and its partner Itera controlling stakes in the segment of the new pipeline that runs through Armenian territory.

Moscow has also consistently attempted to thwart efforts by Central Asian gas producers to enter European gas markets without transiting Russian territory, allowing Russia to maintain crucial leverage. Indeed, these states not only are kept bottled up, but are forced to sell their natural gas to Moscow, which resells it to the European market at twice the price. Moreover, Russia is dependent on the Central Asian natural gas volumes to meet its supply commitments to Europe.

As part of its policy to block the Central Asian states from entering the European natural gas market, Moscow has opposed the building of a proposed Trans-Caspian natural gas pipeline that would transport natural gas from Central Asia to Azerbaijan and thus feed into Azerbaijan's natural gas export pipeline to Georgia and Turkey. From here, it could be supplied to European markets. The United States has been a staunch supporter of this pipeline, precisely because it would grant the Central Asian gas producers the ability to decrease their dependence on Russia for their gas exports and could increase European energy security through diversification of sources.

Moreover, Russia has exploited periods of domestic instability in Central Asia. It has pushed countries in the region to provide further commitments to sell their gas to Russia instead of for direct export, evidently in exchange for Moscow's commitment not to install forces more loyal to it. Accordingly, immediately following the death of Turkmenistan's president Saparmyrat Niyazov, the new government announced its commitment to sell the bulk of Turkmenistan's gas exports to Russia. In addition, during the spring 2007 family challenge to the rule of Kazakhstan's president Nursultan Nazarbayev, the Kazakhstani government announced its intention to export additional oil and natural gas through Russia. This move dampened the possibility that a trans-

Caspian natural gas export pipeline would feed Central Asian gas into the proposed Nabucco pipeline leading to Europe. Moscow's August 2008 invasion of Georgia also aimed to thwart the establishment of further energy export pipelines through its territory, especially targeted at deterring the Central Asian exporters.

In addition to maintaining its dominance as the major natural gas supplier to Europe, Russia continues to work to expand its activities in distributing and selling gas in European markets. Alexander Medvedev, Gazprom's deputy chairman, has said that the company's goal in Europe is to become "an integrated company producing, selling, and distributing gas in Europe."[26]

In recent years, Moscow has explored the idea of building additional oil and natural gas pipelines to markets in Asia. The major routes that have been explored are a southward pipeline to China and an eastward pipeline to Russia's Pacific coast, which would be a natural outlet for consumption by Japan and South Korea. Despite many discussions, media articles, and wooing attempts by both Japan and China, the pipeline ideas remain on the drawing board. Since the extent of Russia's reserves in east Siberia is still unclear and they are largely unexplored, it is not clear whether the volumes in the area would justify the cost of an additional major export pipeline. Moreover, while it is convenient for Moscow to continue to float the idea as a lever to improve relations with China, it is not expected that Moscow would prefer to build an oil pipeline to China that does not reach international markets and thus would increase its dependence on China. The route toward Japan that would allow Russia to export oil to international markets appears far more feasible. China is still weighing the economic feasibility of importing natural gas from Russia. Since the majority of China's major energy consumption centers are on the east coast of the country, LNG is more attractive financially than a long pipeline from Russia, which would have to snake across most of China's territory to the coastal cities.

While Russia is the world's second-largest producer of oil and in certain months even surpasses Saudi Arabia, the largest, its oil export policy is very different from that of the kingdom. Russia is not a member of OPEC and does not coordinate its production and export policies with the organization. The cartel invited Russia to join, but Moscow declined. Moreover, Saudi Arabia and most of the Gulf exporters seek long-term world dependency on large oil consumption and at times have acted to cool prices to prevent moving to other fuels, such as natural gas. Russia has a much more diversified economy than the Gulf producers and a strong human capital base that will allow other elements of the economy to flourish. The Kremlin thus seeks short-term infusions of oil profits—and high and sustained oil prices—to stimulate other aspects of the economy.

Chapter 8
Europe

The formal integration process that led to the formation of the European Union began with energy cooperation. The first treaty-based organization among the European states was the European Coal and Steel Market (Treaty of Paris, 1951); the second was the European Atomic Energy Community (EURATOM, 1957). The EURATOM Treaty was signed the same day as the Treaty of Rome that established the European Economic Community. Despite the fact that energy was one of the first spheres of common action in postwar Western Europe and a driver for Europe's integration, the EU has not yet adopted a common energy policy and the member states sometimes seem to have an aversion to discussing common energy policies. As a result, until 2007, common EU energy policy generally was discussed within the framework of the union's environmental policies. It is not by chance that the main EU energy policy statements produced in recent years are called "Green Papers." Energy policy is the EU sphere where member governments have remained most national in their outlook, defying the trend toward growing integration (for example, many member states still retain national energy companies).

European Union energy policy is coordinated by the European commissioner for energy, whose position is subordinate to the European Commission's Directorate General for Energy and Transport. In addition to the various EU institutions, most of the member states also cooperate within the framework of the International Energy Agency. Moreover, in recent years NATO has taken up the issues of energy security, environmental challenges, and security of energy infrastructure, giving European states an additional opportunity for policy cooperation.

Despite the lack of coordination on energy policy, the energy supply disputes between Russia and the former Soviet republics of Ukraine, Georgia, and Belarus in the winters of 2006 and 2007 produced a serious debate within the EU over member states' increasing dependency on natural gas supplies from Russia that also saw questioning of Moscow's reliability as a supplier (see Chapter 7 for further analysis). In addition, growing concerns about global climate change have raised calls for a common European energy policy. Still, EU member states have declined to adopt common policies. When EU president Jose Manuel Barroso in 2007 unveiled Europe's plans for reducing climate change and introducing more competition into the energy sector, he said that each member state should decide its own energy policy.[1]

One of the reasons the EU has refrained from adopting a united and comprehensive energy policy is that in most states in continental Europe, energy policy is traditionally an element of economic policy.[2] In the case of Germany, for instance, the Foreign Office has traditionally not been involved in energy policy decision making.[3] In France, however, the head of state takes a major role on energy-related policy.

Moreover, in recent years it is the EU that has undertaken the task of splitting up the production, distribution, and supply chain divisions of the energy companies, with the goal of unbundling electricity and gas supplies, which further limits the public sector's involvement in the energy sphere. This is taking place at the same time that on the supply side, producers are extending their involvement in Europe to distribution and supply, and (especially in Russia) the state has reasserted its command over energy suppliers. Moreover, a private and fragmented market is not capable of dealing with the two major challenges defined by Europe: security of supply and environmental policy.

Spring 2007 seems to have been a milestone on the road toward greater cooperation on energy matters in the EU. In March 2007, the European Council adopted an energy program to increase energy saving and promote climate-friendly energy source use. Among the common commitments adopted by the EU member states were: a cut of 20 percent in the EU's greenhouse gas emissions by 2020, with a willingness to up this goal to 30 percent if the United States, China, and India make parallel pledges; a promise that 20 percent of overall energy use will be supplied by renewable energy sources by 2020; and the establishment of a minimum target of 10 percent for the share of biofuels in overall petrol and diesel consumption by 2020.

Europe's Energy Consumption Patterns

The EU posses relatively scant energy reserves: less than 1 percent of the world's proven oil reserves; 2 percent of the world's proven natural gas reserves; and 4 percent of the world's proven coal. By 2020, two-thirds of Europe's energy consumption is expected to be imported.[4] The EU does, however, have a very high energy-efficiency rate, although a large

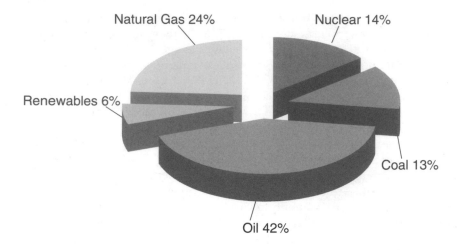

Figure 10. EU TPEC oil (42 percent), natural gas (24 percent), nuclear (14 percent) coal (13 percent), and renewables (6 percent).

gap exists between the veteran EU members and the recent additions from Eastern Europe.

On the other hand, the EU is the second-largest consumer of energy in the world, with 17 percent of the world's total energy consumption in 2003. The EU's total primary energy consumption (TPEC) is comprised of oil (42 percent), natural gas (24 percent), nuclear (14 percent), coal (13 percent), and renewables (6 percent). Its electricity mix is comprised of nuclear (31 percent), coal (30 percent), natural gas (20 percent) and oil (4 percent). Large disparities exist between the patterns of energy use in different member states.

The portion of natural gas in the EU's total primary energy consumption has risen rapidly over the last three decades and will continue to rise. Europe is by far the largest natural gas-importing region in the world and currently importing more natural gas than all other importing regions combined. The fuel is popular in the EU due to its relatively low environmental impact and low cost compared to nuclear or renewable energy sources. Just as Europe's consumption of natural gas is increasing, indigenous natural gas supplies in the EU (North Sea) are rapidly declining. By 2030, Europe will import more than two-thirds of its natural gas, in contrast to a third in 2006. Natural gas use has largely supplanted the use of coal, which has been declining.

The EU member states are split on the issue of nuclear energy. A group of states within the EU—Spain, Portugal, Denmark, and Austria—

opposes nuclear energy. In contrast, France is the second-largest producer of nuclear energy in the world (after the United States); and nuclear energy is the largest share of its energy consumption (39 percent), and close to 80 percent of its electricity consumption is generated by nuclear energy. In addition, the French company Areva is a world leader in the sphere of nuclear energy. The use of nuclear energy is politically contentious in other states like Germany and the United Kingdom, where nuclear energy is in use.

Within the framework of the Kyoto Protocol, the EU has committed to reduce its greenhouse gas emissions by 8 percent from its 1990 levels by 2008–2012. To accomplish this, Europe has initiated a cap-and-trade emissions program though which European companies can meet their commitments by purchasing carbon credits from states with lower or no emissions reductions obligations within the Kyoto Protocol or companies that have succeeded in lowering emissions beyond their obligation. Despite the installation of the cap-and-trade program, the EU has not succeeded in making a dent in the emissions.

As in the United States, the commitment to biofuels seems to have been influenced by the domestic political consideration of creating a market for the European agriculture sector (especially in new members like Poland) rather than policy sensibility. After initial enthusiasm, it seems that Europe's assessment of the utility of biofuels is changing. In light of research published in 2008 that claims that when taking into consideration changes in land use, biofuels should be considered as more hazardous to climate change than helpful, Europe began to question its biofuel policies. In January 2008, the EU began deliberations on banning biofuels grown in forests or in wetlands and grasslands. According to the draft legislation, biofuels used in Europe are required to deliver "a minimum level of greenhouse gas savings,"[5] opening the door to revising its previous policy to encourage production of biofuels.

Europe's Green Paper: The Cornerstone of New Policy

The European Union energy policy and goals are articulated chiefly in the 2006 Green Paper. Preceded by the 2000 Green Paper, it defines three core goals for the EU energy policy: sustainable development, competitiveness, and security of supply.[6] To achieve those goals, the Green Paper identifies six priority areas of action: completion of the internal gas and electricity markets (for example, development of a common European Union energy grid, an improved European interconnection plan, more effective unbundling of the energy networks in Europe); solidarity among member states in ensuring security of supply (such as through legislation on common use of oil and gas stocks and improved transparency of energy stocks at the European level); a sustainable, efficient, diverse energy mix; measures to address the challenges of global warming; research and innovation at the service of Europe's energy policy; and a common external energy plan. As part of this final priority area, the Green Paper states that "Europe needs to speak with a single voice in the international arena"[7] in order to react to the challenges of growing demand, high and volatile energy prices, increasing import dependency, and climate change. The Green Paper states that the EU is the world's second-largest energy market and that "Acting together, . . . has the weight to protect and assert its interests."[8] As the authors correctly point out, a common EU energy policy "would be a break with the past," though "a common European external policy will permit a better integration of energy objectives into broader relations with third countries and policies which support them."[9]

As part of its effort to form a common policy and promote a more activist European approach to the issue, the European Commission is promoting regular presentation of a Strategic EU Energy Review that will be presented to the council and parliament on a regular basis.

As part of its effort to ensure security of supply, the Green Paper states that the EU must promote supply diversity "of energy, country of origin and transit,"[10] focusing on natural gas. It calls for the EU to upgrade and construct new infrastructure to ensure energy security. Examples of this policy would encompass independent (in other words, not through Russia) gas pipelines from the Caspian region, North Africa, and the Middle East and new LNG terminals.

The EU conducts energy dialogues with a number of producer and transit countries. According to the Green Paper, the most notable of these dialogues are with Russia, Norway, Ukraine, the Caspian basin states, Mediterranean countries, OPEC, and the Gulf Cooperation Council. In addition, energy issues are described as a "growing feature" of the EU's political dialogues with other major energy consumers, such as the United States, China, and India.

The Green Paper calls for a new energy initiative with Russia, "the EU's most important energy supplier. The EU, as Russia's largest energy buyer, is an essential and equal partner in this relationship."[11] The document calls for Russia to grant reciprocal access to markets and infrastructure, including in particular third-party access to pipelines. Russian companies enjoy access to bid on ownership in the energy sector in Europe. The EU and Russia have failed to conclude a new EU-Russia Partnership Agreement, despite extensive negotiations, due to disagreement over mutual access to energy pipelines. The Green Paper suggests that EU should make better use of trade policy tools "to promote goals such as nondiscriminatory energy transit and the development of a more secure investment climate."[12] While not mentioned explicitly, it can be assumed that this point is directed toward Russia.

European Energy Security

In Europe, the energy security debates focus on whether and how to diversify natural gas supplies, whether to build more nuclear power plants, and whether to return to (clean) coal. For a number of decades, energy security policy has been a contentious issue between the EU and the United States. During the Cold War, Washington even took measures aimed at preventing the establishment of major export pipelines from the Soviet Union to Europe. The United States has urged Europe to take steps to diversify its energy imports, specifically not to develop dependence on supplies from Russia or its Soviet predecessor. In fact, at times the United States seems to invest more effort than Brussels in promoting European energy security. For example, the United States has been a long-standing proponent of the trans-Caspian pipeline as a means of bringing Central Asian natural gas to Europe, years before Europe became involved in the issue.

The EU has expressed support for additional natural gas pipelines to Europe to decrease its dependence on Russian gas supplies and obtain additional supplies. However, despite its formal support, the pipeline projects have largely been left to the private sector, and the EU has not taken an active role in ensuring that they materialize. Moreover, the EU remains divided over the merits of proposed new pipeline routes. Poland, for example, strongly opposes the German-led North European trans-Baltic pipeline project, which would directly link Russia and Germany, and thus would decrease Russia's dependence on Poland as a transit state for its natural gas exports to Europe. Poland's defense minister Radosław Sikorski has gone so far as to compare the proposed North European pipeline to the 1939 Nazi-Soviet Molotov-Ribbentrop Pact that carved up Eastern Europe between the two powers.[13]

The EU's ability to minimize its risks from its extensive gas imports from Russia and to create interdependency between supplier and consumer is undermined by both the lack of unity in EU dealings with Russia and the behavior of individual European companies. Instead of acting in unison, each state or company within a state cuts a separate deal with Gazprom. If the EU were to act as a united market, Gazprom would also be dependent on Europe. But an individual market cannot create such an interdependent relationship with Russia. Instead, the states and individual companies compete with each other for Gazprom's supplies and routes.

The EU now plans to foster greater competition by fragmenting its energy markets. Gazprom, unintentionally, may be more a benefactor of this process than European consumers. While European companies face legal bars to consolidation, Gazprom has been entering the distribution market in a number of EU countries and uniting the functions of producer and distributor while remaining Europe's leading source of natural gas. Moreover, some European companies have formed cooperation agreements with Gazprom—at times not transparently—in order to preserve the two functions. The European Union's ability to defend itself from Gazprom's acquisition of both supply and distribution functions is compromised by the fact that many European companies have undercut the EU efforts. In return for long-term supplies, these distribution companies have offered Gazprom access to their local marketing business, essentially leaving the two functions in hands that are intertwined.[14]

While Gazprom has access to the supply and distribution markets in the EU, there is no reciprocity for EU companies in Russia. Reciprocity could enhance interdependency between the two sides and thus enhance the EU energy security. Former Russian president Vladimir Putin's refusal to allow European companies access to the Russian distribution system and transport pipelines has become a thorn in Russia's dealing with the EU, and specifically with German underchancellor Angela Merkel. The European Union competition commissioner has said that Moscow must grant access to its gas pipelines: "We are seeking a level playing field, a win-win for both sides."[15]

Policy Implications: Reducing Vulnerability

To achieve enhanced energy security, Europe will have to take advantage of its size and act as a single customer. Small markets in Europe will be more vulnerable to supply disruptions and political pressure than would a large united market. Moreover, Russia in its energy dealings is investor, landlord, and regulator. If Europe is going to deal with Russia on the supply side, it must take advantage of its potential strength and size as a united energy market.

Since 2006, Moscow through a variety of regulatory schemes has progressively pushed foreign companies out of upstream gas exploration and production ventures in Russia. Moreover, Russia has refused to open its supply and distribution networks to foreign companies. Importers of Gazprom's gas should demand reciprocity in the sphere of investment in upstream and downstream ventures of Russian energy supplies and demand that Russia join the European energy charter as a condition for it serving as Europe's dominant natural gas supplier.

Chapter 9
The United States

Because it is the world's largest energy consumer and economy, the United States has more impact on global energy trends than any other country. Indeed, not only is the United States the world's largest energy consumer, it is also the largest energy producer and net importer. The United States possesses the world's largest coal reserves, sixth-largest natural gas reserves, and eleventh-largest oil reserves. It is also the second-largest producer of climate-altering gases, and the largest on a per capita basis.[1]

Energy policy is integrated thoroughly into U.S. foreign and national security policies, and Washington frequently uses energy sanctions and policies as a tool to advance policies. For decades, the United States has approached energy security from a global perspective. In an integrated world oil market, securing supplies for its own market does not grant immunity from the economic costs of high world oil prices. As a global commodity, imported or domestically produced oil costs the same to U.S. consumers. Thus, Washington has traditionally tended to work to bring more oil to world markets, not just to its own shores. In addition, the United States views ensuring reliable energy supplies to its allies as an integral part of security guarantees. Domestic political discussions in recent years have also emphasized energy independence as a factor in energy security, in contrast to the previous approach. In a poll conducted in 2006, Americans described "energy dependence" as their second greatest concern after the war in Iraq.[2] Accordingly, President George W. Bush and other officials joined those calling for reduction of oil imports, not just oil use. For example, in his January 2006 State of the Union address, Bush called for reducing oil imports from the Middle East by 75 percent by 2025. In his official campaign materials, President Obama called for eliminating oil imports from Venezuela and the Middle East within ten years. Moreover, in candidates' statements from all parts of the political spectrum in the 2008 U.S. presidential elections, it seems that the concepts of energy security and energy independence became blurred, despite their questionable connection.

The bulk of U.S. oil imports arrive and are processed at installations in states along the shore of the Gulf of Mexico. More than one-third of U.S. oil production comes from the Gulf Coast and the offshore waters between Alabama and Texas, and more than 50 percent of U.S. refining capacity is located in the same region. Hurricanes Katrina and Rita in 2005 illustrated to Washington that not only can global energy supplies be threatened by disruptions in critical producer states and important naval chokepoints, such as the Hormuz and Malacca Straits, but supplies that have reached the Gulf of Mexico are vulnerable to the whims of Mother Nature. Washington has not yet succeeded in providing a policy answer to this vulnerability.

Background: U.S. Energy Use

Possession of expansive energy resources fueled the development of the U.S. economy during the nineteenth and first half of the twentieth century. Unlike most oil and gas producers today, the United States decided in the nineteenth century that the private sector rather than the government should own natural resource commodities. The central government also established a strong system that upheld property rights over energy resources, which helped attract investments in this sector. More than 80 percent of U.S. reserves are concentrated in four states: Texas (22 percent), Louisiana (20 percent), Alaska (20 percent), and California (18 percent). Oil played a significant role in the economic and social development of these states.

The 1970s oil crisis fundamentally changed the way the United States consumes oil. Until the 1970s, oil was an all-purpose fuel. In contrast, today it is primarily a transportation fuel, with 65 percent of consumption used for transportation. Other parts of the economy, especially manufacturing, switched to alternative fuels such as natural gas. U.S. consumers also used technology to increase energy efficiency immensely. Consequently, today the United States uses half the amount of oil per dollar of GDP compared to the 1970s.

Since oil is now a less important input to the economy, the United States is able to sustain higher oil prices longer before recession kicks in. This ability to tolerate high oil prices also means that U.S. consumption is less affected by price hikes than in the past, and thus prices are likely to stay high for longer periods. In addition, high oil prices have a mixed impact on the U.S. economy. Increased wealth is transferred abroad to pay for oil imports, but U.S.-based oil companies and oil-related industries (drilling, engineering, transport) benefit.

While the relative role of oil in U.S. fuel consumption has declined dramatically since the 1970s, actual volumes of oil consumption have grown because of the country's population and economic growth. Moreover, domestic production is declining, so net oil imports have climbed steadily in recent decades. In 1973, the United States imported 35 percent of the oil it consumed; in 2007 it imported close to 60 percent. The bulk of U.S. oil imports come from Canada, Mexico, Saudi Arabia, Venezuela, and Nigeria.

The United States has the largest oil-refining capacity in the world. However, this capacity has not significantly grown in three decades: no new oil refineries have been built in the United States since the 1970s, although capacity has been expanded at existing refineries. In the fall of 2005, the vulnerability of U.S. refining capacity was exposed when Hurricanes Katrina and Rita paralyzed refineries throughout the Gulf Coast region.

The United States is the second-largest producer of coal in the world, after China. It also widely consumes coal, especially for electricity generation; nearly 50 percent of the electricity produced in the United States is generated from coal. This sector consumes 90 percent of the coal used in the United States. Representatives from coal-producing states and coal industry lobbies consequently have significant impact on energy policy outcomes.

In recent decades, another significant trend in the United States has been the rapid growth of natural gas consumption, which has increased by approximately 20 percent since 1990. Natural gas is used in the United States mainly in the industrial (38 percent), electric power (24 percent), residential (22 percent), and commercial (13 percent) sectors. Liquid natural gas imports are also rising significantly and are expected to grow further in the coming decades.

Immediately after the 1973 oil crisis, nuclear power use grew rapidly in the United States, but within a few years it subsided; the last new order for a nuclear plant was in 1978, and this plant was ultimately canceled. Some companies have recently indicated interest in moving forward with new facilities. The United States continues to be the world's largest producer of nuclear energy, and American companies are leading exporters of nuclear power plants. Approximately 20 percent of U.S. electricity is generated by nuclear power. Wind, solar, biomass, and geothermal power, although growing, continue to supply only a tiny fraction of total energy consumption in the United States.

Energy as an Element of U.S. Foreign and National Security Policy

Energy is an integrated policy tool in U.S. foreign policy, and energy security is a clear goal of national security policy. Due to the massive scale of both its energy production and consumption, the United States is uniquely positioned to affect energy policy globally and in a variety of regional settings.

While the potential use of the oil weapon by producing states is frequently discussed, the United States in fact has used its role as the leading consumer to wield the oil weapon against energy exporters. Denial of markets has been used far more frequently in recent decades than denial of supplies by producers. Since August 1996, the United States has imposed mandatory and discretionary sanctions within the framework of the Iran-Libya Sanctions Act (ILSA) on companies that invest more than $20 million annually (lowered in August 1997 from $40 million) in the Iranian oil and natural gas sectors.[3] In April 2004, Washington removed Libya from ILSA sanctions after deciding that Libya was committed to ridding itself of weapons of mass destruction and had renounced terrorism. The United States maintains sanctions on two oil-producing states in addition to Iran: Sudan and Syria (in Sudan, aimed at stopping human rights violations and genocide; in Syria, formally due to its support for terrorism, but most likely due to its assistance to representatives of the Saddam Hussein regime that found refuge in Syria). Furthermore, prior to the U.S. invasion of Iraq in 2003, UN sanctions were imposed on Iraq's oil exports, and the United States served as the main power imposing and enforcing them.

The United States openly promotes oil and natural gas pipeline routes as a means to cement political and security relations. This policy can be seen in Washington's promotion during the 1990s of the Baku-Tbilisi-Ceyhan pipeline to export Caspian oil and natural gas (for more on the U.S. involvement in promoting this project, see Chapter 3). Moreover, Washington strives to reduce the dependencies of its allies on Russia and other natural gas exporters through promoting multiple natural gas supply sources. Since the beginning of European gas imports from the Soviet Union in the late 1970s, Washington has been prodding Europe to take on additional major gas suppliers. In recent years, the United States has actively promoted establishment of a trans-Caspian pipeline to supply Central Asian natural gas to European markets, illustrating its concern for European energy security on an issue that has no direct bearing on U.S. energy security.

The Strategic Petroleum Reserve

One of the most important tools in Washington's arsenal for impacting world oil trends is its strategic petroleum reserve (SPR). The SPR was established on the heels of the 1970s oil crisis. Formally inaugurated in December 1975, when Congress passed the Energy Policy and Conservation Act (EPCA), the reserve can hold up to a billion barrels of oil. In 2007, the SPR held 700 million barrels, making it the largest emergency oil stockpile in the world. The SPR is organized so that it can meet U.S. oil needs for 90 days. In 2007 the Bush administration called for Congress to double the capacity as part of policy efforts to increase US energy security.[4]

Under the EPCA legislation, there is no preset "trigger" for withdrawing oil from the SPR. Instead, the president determines that drawdown is required by "a severe energy supply interruption or by obligations of the United States" to the International Energy Agency. EPCA defines a "severe energy supply interruption" as one that (1) "is, or is likely to be, of significant scope and duration, and of an emergency nature"; (2) "may cause major adverse impact on national safety or the national economy" (including an oil price spike); or (3) "results, or is likely to result, from an interruption in the supply of imported petroleum products, or from sabotage or an act of God."

The reserve's very existence adds an element of security to the world oil market. In addition, through release of supplies at critical junctures, Washington has been able to affect world oil price trends. Even verbal threats to release volumes from the SPR have allowed Washington to moderate OPEC's behavior and calm world oil markets. U.S. energy policy experts differ, however, as to the appropriate function of the reserve: whether it is to be used only to prevent supply disruptions, or as a tool to moderate oil prices.

Formation of U.S. Energy Policy: All Policies Are Local

Despite the prominent place of energy policies in U.S. official documents and debates, energy policy in the United States remains uncoordinated and often driven by local interests. U.S. decision-making on energy is quite decentralized: it is divided among different government agencies; federal, state, and local governments; and different regulatory authorities that at times promote conflicting policies. Moreover, the private sector takes the lead in a number of areas related to energy policy. In addition, U.S.-based oil companies in recent decades have distanced themselves from Washington's agenda and policies. Accordingly, in analyzing U.S. policy stances, one needs to separate those of U.S.-based energy companies and those of the U.S. government.

The impact of domestic politics on U.S. energy policies, including those with international implications, is evident in a number of areas. In 1980, a *Washington Post* article eloquently summarized the inconsistencies produced in U.S. energy policies due to domestic considerations:

Consider this anomaly. The president and a great many more Americans are prepared to talk openly of war to secure the oil routes out of the Gulf. But neither the president nor many others are ready to impose a tax on gasoline to diminish imports that, everyone agrees, constitute a clear and present danger to national security.[5]

Indeed, despite the great contribution that higher gasoline taxes and stricter fuel efficiency standards have made in slowing down the growth of oil use in Europe and other countries, the United States has refrained from adopting these policies out of fear of domestic political retribution. U.S. fuel efficiency standards, known as Corporate Average Fuel Economy (CAFE), are among the lowest in industrialized states; even those of developing states like China are significantly higher. Raising fuel efficiency in vehicles to Japanese and European levels could decrease the amount of oil consumed in the United States by approximately 5 million barrels a day (of a total 20 million)—with no technological advances required. However, it was only in December 2007 that the White House signed a bill into law that raises the U.S. CAFE standards for the first time in thirty-two years. This same bill also establishes new efficiency requirements for household appliances and government buildings and sets a goal of phasing out the incandescent light bulb within ten years.

During the 2008 U.S. presidential election campaigns, U.S. energy security policies occupied an exceptionally prominent place. However, the plans of President Obama and Senator McCain did not differ significantly. Most candidates, including Obama, supported reducing U.S. imports of foreign oil, even though that does not make oil consumption more affordable or enhance U.S. or global energy security. Traditionally, presidential candidates who have voiced support for energy policies that threaten the U.S. coal industry or automakers have generally lost the elections. In the 2000 election, Al Gore is believed to have lost traditionally Democratic party-leaning coal-producing states such as West Virginia because he was perceived as supporting legislation that would impose limitations on the use of coal in the United States.

The Politics of Biofuels

Despite general U.S. belief that the market should drive the direction of innovation, the federal government, especially Congress, has determined some of the winners and losers of the scientific game with its decisions to subsidize certain industries and research directions. This is quite evident in the sphere of energy. Washington's choices in promoting various alternative energy sources and research on them is often dictated by domestic interests. Moreover, despite an American preference for open trade, Congress at times imposes tariffs on energy imports. The politics surrounding corn-based ethanol exemplify both trends.

The Bush administration chose promotion of production and consumption of ethanol as a tool to address the challenge of climate change and U.S. dependence on oil imports. This approach was puzzling since the leading biofuel produced in the United States, corn-based ethanol, produces only a minor net energy gain and little if any improvement in net carbon emissions. Most optimistic sources claim that the net energy gain from using biofuels over petroleum is a reduction of 20 percent of oil consumption, because of the intensive use of petroleum products in agriculture and the need to truck biofuels to fueling stations. Furthermore, use of ethanol as opposed to petroleum reduces climate-altering gases at best by 13 percent. Some scientists believe that if land-use change is taken into account, production of biofuels actually exacerbates climate change. Clearing natural vegetation to make way for biofuel crops also deprives the planet of "sponges" that absorb carbon. And burning vegetation to clear fields also has a negative impact on climate change. This has been especially evident in developing countries that have initiated biofuels projects, such as Indonesia and Brazil. In addition, biofuel groups require increases in water usage, which also raises energy consumption. Support for corn-based ethanol has another drawback: it does not give a fair chance for the development of other sources of ethanol that seem to offer more promise than their corn-based cousin. For example, the U.S. government gives a special tax credit of 51 cents a gallon for ethanol. But it has placed a tariff of 54 cents per gallon on ethanol imported from Brazil. This is despite the fact that Brazil's fuel is produced from sugarcane, which provides a far greater energy gain than corn.

U.S. policies on ethanol are probably best explained by the input of U.S. domestic politics and interests on Washington's energy policies. Corn is grown in the United States in electorally important states such as Iowa, and so perhaps it is not surprising that corn-based ethanol receives unparalleled government support and subsidies. In his 2007 State of the Union address, President Bush called for ethanol to replace 20 percent of U.S. gasoline consumption in twenty years. Members of Congress from corn-growing states have been at the forefront of efforts to preserve the subsidies for ethanol and the tariff on Brazilian imports. Despite the many government agencies and institutions that deal intensively with energy policy, Washington has yet to succeed in creating an energy policy focusing on U.S. national security interests: instead, these policies are driven primarily by the interests of various domestic concerns.

An important challenge for the U.S. government is to craft appropriate policy initiatives to stimulate innovation in the sphere of energy. Washington needs to provide incentives that will foster development of new sources of energy and energy-use conservation measures, without determining itself what those measures should be.[6]

Chapter 10
China

China's energy consumption patterns and policies have attracted widespread international interest. This is not surprising: China's consumption accounts for close to half the growth in world oil consumption in the last decade. This growth has transformed China into a major energy importer and helped fuel the run-up in international oil prices in the early twenty-first century. But it also reflects three other factors: the vast scale of China's energy production and consumption; uncertainty over future trends in China's energy policies; and the broader security, economic, and political implications of China's choices and behavior for the international system.

China is the world's second-largest consumer of energy. It is the world's largest producer and consumer of coal, second-largest importer and consumer of oil, and second-largest producer of electricity. However, China's energy consumption mix differs significantly from that of most industrialized countries: 70 percent coal and only a comparatively small amount of oil and natural gas. China is as a result the world's largest producer of greenhouse gases. Heavy consumption of coal has also generated tremendous environmental and health problem problems for the country domestically. This is particularly so because coal and solid biomass are in widespread use in home stoves, exposing hundreds of millions of people to indoor pollutants. The majority of China's rural population regularly use solid coal and biomass for heating and cooking.

China's energy production is very limited, with officials preferring to produce electricity cheaply and quickly with coal. In a 2007 energy document, the government declared its intention to expand its nuclear energy production.

The bulk of indigenous sources of energy in China are located far from the major centers of consumption on the southeast coast. Thus, a major task of Chinese energy policies is internal distribution. In addition, China has very low energy efficiency, consuming 50 percent more

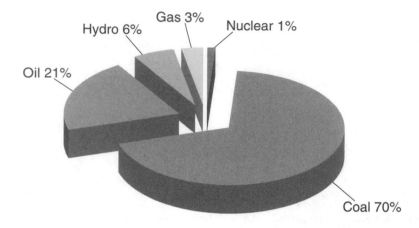

Figure 11. China's TCP graph. Coal (70 percent), oil (21 percent), hydroelectric (6 percent), natural gas (3 percent), nuclear (1 percent).

energy per dollar of GNP than advanced industrial countries. As stated in its official energy doctrine, published in 2007, due to low energy efficiency, with "an increase solely in supply [it] is hard to meet the rising demand for energy."[1] The document identified additional problems in China's energy sector: "Coal production safety is far from satisfactory, the structure of power grids is not rational, the oil reserves are not sufficient, and an effective emergency pre-warning system is yet to be improved and consolidated to deal with energy supply breakdowns and other major unexpected emergencies."[2]

Because the Kyoto Protocol focused on developed economies, China is currently under no international obligations to reduce greenhouse gas emissions. Nor has China voluntarily undertaken major policy measures to reduce them. Indeed, Beijing has acted in international forums such as the UN Security Council to prevent attempts to force such policy changes.

The year 1993 marked a turning point for China: for the first time, its oil consumption exceeded its domestic production, and thus China joined the world's oil importers. Subsequently, it has gone from self-sufficiency to importing half its total oil supply. To be sure, China still ranks as the world's sixth-largest oil producer. The veteran oil and gas fields are found in and around Daqing and Shengli in northeast China, but their production is either flat or declining. The center of new production is in the Tarim basin in the northwest region of Xinjiang. This region is inhabited largely by ethnic minorities of Muslim descent, many of whom share ethnic and family ties with ethnic groups in bordering states such as Kazakhstan and Kyrgyzstan. Energy production in this province has led to an economic boost for the region, but has also encouraged the arrival of a large number of ethnic majority Chinese, affecting the delicate demographic balance in the region and, potentially, its stability.

In its approach to the three elements of energy security—reliability of supply, affordability, and friendliness to the environment—Beijing gives priority to reliability of supply over the other two elements. Thus, Beijing encourages its oil companies to gain ownership of energy supplies and infrastructure around the globe, at times even at the expense of economic rationality. The government goal of preventing dependence on the international market for energy supplies often leads China to adopt these non-market-driven energy policy decisions. If continued, this approach to energy security could place a brake on economic growth. The growth rate of energy use already outpaces GDP growth. China's obsession with security of supply seems puzzling since it has sufficient domestic oil production to ensure that in a crisis it will have enough supplies for its military and other essential state functions.

Acting on the dictate of the country's de facto leader, Deng Xiaoping, Chinese oil companies in 1993 initiated a policy of "going out" and acquiring concession rights in oil fields abroad. This brought Chinese oil companies to a number of oil-producing states, including some—such as Sudan and Myanmar—to which Western oil companies have limited access due to U.S. sanctions on the governing regimes.[3] U.S. officials and some European representatives have expressed concerns that China's investments in these rogue states help sustain these regimes, undermining international efforts to coerce them to change their policies or to bring about regime change.

The United States has also undertaken other efforts to limit the reach of China's oil companies. In 2005, Washington blocked an attempt by China's CNOOC oil company to acquire the American oil major Unocal. In addition, Washington took steps in the last decade to limit Chinese participation in a number of major oil production projects in Kazakhstan. The U.S. effort to block Chinese entry into a number of regions reinforces the views of those in China who promote an aggressive policy to enhance supply reliability, claiming that they are not allowed full access to the international oil market.

Beijing and Washington have also clashed at times over how to deal with Iran and other Middle East oil producers, but their interests are actually more congruent than divergent. China's transformation to an energy importer means that, like the United States, it has acquired an interest in stability in the Persian Gulf region and preserving ruling regimes in the oil producers to prevent supply disruptions. For example,

China wants neither the emergence of a nuclear-armed Iran nor war in the region to prevent it. At the end of the day, China will most likely not undermine international efforts to defuse the Iranian nuclear weapons program.

While Chinese oil companies' acquisitions of foreign oil and gas assets have received considerable international attention, their impact on Chinese oil imports is still meager. Most Chinese oil projects abroad are in the form of production-sharing agreements with local national companies in which the companies receive revenue, not equity oil. Thus, they do not directly promote the government's goal of enhanced reliability of supply. In 2005, China's assets abroad generated less than 300,000 barrels a day of oil imported to China, less than 8.5 percent of Beijing's total oil imports.[4] In addition, the Chinese companies do not ship their entire equity oil home, preferring to sell it on international markets to customers closer to the production sites. Furthermore, many of the sites where Chinese companies are active produce oil that is unsuitable for China's refineries.

Moreover, contracts and control of equity oil overseas cannot guarantee supplies, especially in a security crunch. If an economic blockade were imposed on China or there were security impediments in major sea lanes, legal possession of equity oil from overseas would not help get it home. Indeed, growing oil imports have only increased China's reliance on U.S. maintenance of open access through world sea lanes and major chokepoints. Over four-fifths of China's oil imports pass through the vulnerable Malacca Strait, making Beijing highly dependent on its stability.

Over the last decade, China has steadily increased its relative share of oil imports from Russia and other Caspian states and decreased the portion from the Middle East. But the bulk of China's oil imports still come from the Middle East. In addition, a third of China's oil imports are supplied by African states, with Angola the largest supplier. While China has extensive oil-refining capability, it has limited capacity to process many of the Middle Eastern heavy oil grades, such as those supplied by Saudi Arabia.

Chinese officials have begun to grasp that their current policy may not be doing as much for energy security as they thought and are beginning to question their approach. Purchases of oil from spot markets are growing, but according to its 2007 energy document, Beijing wants to curb this trend and rely less on market exchanges and more on long-term contracts. These types of supply relations, in contrast to spot market exchanges, tend to create more opportunity for interaction between political policies and energy exchanges.

In addition, during the last decade China has explored and promoted a long list of options for building international pipelines to import oil and natural gas. Still, only one international pipeline—from Kazakhstan—has been built to China. This oil pipeline, which became operational in late 2006, is unique, since it does not lead to world markets, but only supplies China (see Chapter 3 for more extensive discussion of this pipeline). While China is exploring a number of natural gas import pipelines from the greater Caspian region, commercial considerations make it unlikely that most will materialize. As we noted, major centers of energy consumption in China are located on the east coast, far from domestic and Caspian gas sources, meaning that long domestic pipelines would be needed to transport Caspian gas to Chinese consumers. Thus, it seems more likely that China will expand its liquid natural gas imports, which should prove more commercially attractive than long-haul pipeline imports.

The precise process by which China's energy policies are formed is unclear and seems in flux, with different government ministries and the oil companies playing strong roles. The publication of the comprehensive energy policy document in 2007 is an attempt to conceptualize and provide a guideline for new energy policies. China does not have an energy ministry that is tasked with coordinating government policy in this sphere. Policy toward activities abroad is strongly influenced by China's oil companies, which are principally motivated by commercial considerations. Although largely government owned, they succeed in swaying many energy policies, including determining foreign venues for exploration and investment. Accordingly, not all the activities of Chinese oil companies abroad should be viewed as an expression of Beijing's national policies. The interests of the companies do not entirely overlap with those of the government and at times even conflict. The companies may exploit their advantage in knowledge of international energy dealings to promote their own interests, which they present as promoting government interests. At the same time, the Chinese government does not expect them to run as primarily commercial enterprises, and does not always allow the companies to enjoy the fruits of their successes.

There is great uncertainty as to future trends in China's energy consumption, since the government has yet to form comprehensive energy policies. Energy prices, including for finished petroleum products, are kept below international market rates, and the domestic energy sector is also heavily regulated. This situation gives little incentive to Chinese energy companies to increase domestic production and little incentive for the consumer to reduce consumption. In its 2007 energy document, Beijing stated it hopes to reform the pricing system for its domestic energy supplies.

An important factor in China's energy consumption is state subsidies. Reduction of some gasoline consumption subsidies in summer 2008 produced significant results in reducing consumption. Further reduction or elimination of state energy subsidies would be an effective means to further consumption trends and will have an impact on international oil prices.

China can quite easily make great leaps in energy efficiency. High oil prices will motivate it to acquire and develop technologies that will enable it to do this. An additional measure that may sate China's drive for oil supply assurances is its development of strategic reserves, which could provide the confidence to rely more heavily on market supplies of oil. This may take place in coordination or even formal association with the International Energy Agency. China's association with the organization is under discussion within the organization and in dialogues between leading member states and China.

Chapter 11
Iran

Iran's energy profile is unique: the country possesses the second-largest proven reserves of natural gas and is the world's fourth-largest producer of oil. At the same time, Iran has no major natural gas export projects, and imports more natural gas than it exports. In addition, over 40 percent of oil production is consumed in the domestic market, and Iran imports close to half its gasoline consumption. Moreover, Tehran is a net importer of electricity. Iran has a modest refining capacity, and thus spends a large portion of its state budget on imported petroleum products. According to President Mahmoud Ahmadinejad, gasoline subsidies cost Iran $5 billion in 2006. The International Monetary Fund estimates that energy subsidies cost the government $20 billion annually, about 15 percent of Iran's economic output, and contribute to very low energy efficiency. To address the rising expense of subsidies, Tehran in May 2007 announced a decision to ration subsidized gasoline. The policy was met by widespread public outrage, including acts of violence against government institutions and gasoline stations.

Iran's economy and state budget are highly dependent on revenue from oil exports. Hydrocarbons account for over a fifth of Iran's GDP. Oil revenues make up approximately 80 percent of total export earnings and 40 to 50 percent of government revenue. Ahmadinejad was elected in 2005 on the slogan, "To put oil revenues on every table," which increased public expectations for additional government expenditures. Yet massive government spending has led to a situation in which little money is left for reinvestment in Iran's oil and gas production, which has created a large gap between the size of Iran's oil and gas reserves and its production capacity.

Iran's unique energy profile can be explained in part by its large population of over 70 million, which, consumes over 70 percent of the country's gas production. Oil producers with large populations, like Iran, are particularly vulnerable to price fluctuations, having less ability to reduce government spending during periods of lower oil revenues. Iran established a national oil fund—the Oil Stabilization Fund (OSF)—in December 2000 with the aim of using it to cushion the government budget from revenue changes resulting from international oil price fluctuations.

The Islamic Republic of Iran is a classic energy export rentier state: political power is sustained by massive government spending derived from the revenues from energy exports. Harvard sociologist Theda Skocpol based her important work on rentier states on Iran.[1] Skocpol anticipated that regardless of the orientation of the regime, its sustenance through oil revenues would shape its basic structure. During the early days of the Islamic Republic, Skocpol commented:

> Prerevolutionary Iran was . . . a rentier state, where revenues from exports of oil and natural gas were channeled by the state, not so much into truly productive economic investments, but instead into lavish purchases of modern armaments and into elite luxury consumption. An Iranian Islamic Republic could remain, for quite some time, another sort of rentier state: a populist, welfare-oriented rentier state, with the ulama passing out alms in return for moral conformity on a grander scale than ever before. Unemployment and underemployment could continue at high levels in a stagnant national economy.[2]

In the last decade, government spending in Iran has been progressively expanding, quadrupling since 1999. The power and ability to provide goods and jobs, despite the lack of production in the economy, contributes to the longevity of the Islamic Republic.

The Iranian energy sector is controlled completely by the state. The National Iranian Oil Company (NIOC) and its subsidiary companies perform the majority of the functions in the hydrocarbon sector: exploration, production, distribution, and export. The Iranian constitution bars granting foreigners rights to oil and natural gas production on a concessionary basis or with a direct equity stake. Therefore, despite its vast untapped energy wealth, Iran is not nearly as attractive a target for foreign investment in the energy sector as it would be otherwise. To circumvent its constitutional limitations, Iran has instituted a system of buyback contracts that grant investors the right to purchase particular percentages of a field's produced oil or gas. The buyback system has major disadvantages for both Iran and the foreign investors. By offering a fixed rate of return, NIOC bears all the risk of low oil prices. The foreign companies do not receive rights to develop or operate their discoveries, factors that affect production outcomes and profits. Finally, companies are generally not attracted to the short-term aspect of the buyback contracts and the fixed financial terms that limit potential payback. Thus, within the buyback framework, foreign oil companies basically operate as contractors for the government for a limited time.

Oil

As we noted, Iran is the world's fourth largest producer of oil; it has the third-largest proven oil reserves and is the third-largest oil exporter. The bulk of Iran's oil production is in Khuzestan province, adjacent to the border with Iraq. Over 40 percent of Iran's oil production is consumed domestically.[3] In 2005, Iran produced 4.05 million barrels per day, significantly below the average levels of production in the years before the 1979 Islamic Revolution, and less than that of producers with significantly smaller proven reserves, such as Russia. Due to the extensive use of oil revenues for government spending, Tehran does not invest much in renewing and expanding production. With sufficient investment, Iran could increase its crude oil production capacity significantly. Economic geographer Roger Stern claims, however, that at the current rate of declining production and rising domestic consumption, Iran could become an oil importer by the year 2015.[4]

Domestic oil consumption in Iran is inadvertently encouraged by government subsidies. Until the implementation of rationing in June 2007, Iranians had almost unlimited access to gasoline at a price at the pump of a mere 35 cents a gallon, less than 10 cents a liter—five times below world gasoline rates. These subsidies have been especially costly to the government, since Iran has limited refining capacity of light fuels. There were 9 oil refineries in 2008, most built before the 1979 revolution. Thus, Iran imports over 40 percent of its gasoline consumption, making it the second-largest gasoline importer after the United States. Consequently, the government is not only spending a large part of its revenue on domestic energy subsidies, but paying for the refining abroad. In addition, until fuel rationing began, a large amount of fuel was smuggled to neighboring states, meaning that Tehran inadvertently had been subsidizing foreign consumers.

Given its extreme dependence on oil revenues to sustain the state budget, Iran, like many oil producers with large populations, prefers that OPEC carry out policies that sustain high oil prices. In contrast, oil exporters with smaller populations, such as the majority of the Gulf states, often promote policies that lead to moderate oil prices, in order to ensure long-term oil demand.

Natural Gas

Even though it has the world's second-largest proven reserves of natural gas (only Russia has more), Iran is a net importer and has no liquid natural gas or major pipeline export projects. Iran exports limited amounts of natural gas to Turkey (in 2005, 4.32 bcm, billion cubic meters) and Armenia. It imports gas from Azerbaijan and Turkmenistan for consumption in its northern cities, and some of this gas is reexported to Armenia. Technically, both the Armenian and Turkish pipelines could be extended to serve as a venue to move Iranian natural gas to European markets. Iran's largest gas field is the South Pars field, which is shared with Qatar, the world's largest exporter of LNG.

The main domestic uses of natural gas are for reinjection into oil wells and for electricity generation; it is also used as a home heating fuel. As for gasoline, the price of natural gas is heavily subsidized and this has promoted rapid growth in domestic demand.

Nuclear Energy

Iran is developing a nuclear energy program, the center of which is a light water Russian-built reactor at the city of Bushehr. Tehran would like to attain control of the complete nuclear fuel-processing cycle, including fuel production. Due to a number of violations of its nuclear safeguard obligations with the International Atomic Energy Agency, including clandestine acquisition of components of its nuclear program from Pakistan's A. Q. Khan network and findings of undeclared nuclear material, a number of governments in the world claim that Tehran is operating a parallel nuclear weapons program.[5] This claim is boosted by the fact that it is clearly not economically sensible for Iran to be developing nuclear energy rather than producing electricity from its domestic gas supplies. The Bushehr plant is not yet in operation, partly because of commercial disagreements with Russia and also because of technical challenges. In addition, international sanctions are progressively being increased against Iran, with the goal of forcing it to comply with measures that would limit its nuclear capability.

The Energy Trade and Foreign Relations

Tehran's failure to establish any major natural gas export project is an indication of its strategic isolation. Iran hopes to become a significant supplier to European gas markets. It is the only state in Europe's proximity with sufficient proven volumes that it could offset Europe's dependence on Moscow's gas supplies. Accordingly, Iran's and Russia's interests clash in the sphere of natural gas supplies.

Iran has territorial disputes with most of its neighbors that could affect its oil and gas production and export. There are disputes with Qatar over exploitation of the South Pars/North Dome field, with the

UAE over control of the Abu Musa and Tunb Islands, and with other countries on the Caspian Sea over Caspian delimitation.[6]

Tehran often blames U.S. sanctions for deterring foreign companies and states from entering into investment and supply agreements with Iran in the energy sector. However, many company representatives who have attempted to establish projects in Iran say that the real impediments to foreign investment are the unfavorable business climate in Iran, the inability to purchase exploration and production rights, and the widespread bureaucracy and corruption.[7]

While Iran has not succeeded in forging major natural gas export projects, it does maintain significant oil supply contracts with a number of states, especially in Asia. Iran supplies Japan with over half a million of barrels a day and China with close to 300,000. Tehran also conducts oil export-swapping agreements with landlocked Kazakhstan and Turkmenistan and on a limited basis with Azerbaijan. The swaps involve delivery of Caspian oil to the Iranian town of Neka on the Caspian Sea for processing and consumption in northern Iran. In return, an equivalent amount of oil is exported by Iran through Persian Gulf terminals, for which the exporters receive payment. The swaps are facilitated by a pipeline from Neka to Tehran, with a spur to Tabriz (which has a refinery). The swaps are modest: in 2006, they amounted to approximately 120,000 barrels a day. More important than the volume is the fact that the United States has not actively opposed this trade and has not declared it in violation of U.S. legislation limiting trade with Iran.

In its showdown with the international community over its nuclear program, fears have been raised that Tehran could decide to stop its oil exports and upset the flow of oil in the Strait of Hormuz. However, as is seen in this analysis, Iran itself is especially vulnerable to economic sanctions of this type. First, the state budget is entirely dependent on revenue from oil export. And second, Tehran requires imports for most of its gasoline consumption. Accordingly, Iran is dependent on free flow of traffic through the Strait of Hormuz to guarantee its ability to export oil and import gasoline.

Prospects for a Gas Cartel?

Iran is at the forefront of efforts to establish a natural gas producers' cartel. Venezuela stands with Iran in efforts to promote the formation of this cartel and like Iran is not yet a major gas exporter. Major natural gas producers meet regularly in the framework of the Gas Exporting Countries Forum (GECF) for consultations, but have not adopted any measures for formal coordination. The founding ministerial meeting of the GECF was held in Tehran in May 2001. Members include Algeria,

Bolivia, Brunei, Egypt, Indonesia, Iran, Libya, Malaysia, Oman, Qatar, Russia, Trinidad and Tobago, the UAE, and Venezuela. In February 2007, Iranian supreme leader Ali Khamenei suggested that Russia and Iran could establish "an organization of gas cooperation like OPEC."[8] Since Iran has no major gas export projects, it has little to lose from efforts to regulate export in order to improve the power and profits of the natural gas producers.

The prospects for forming a functioning natural gas cartel do not appear good at this point. Russia's full participation in the effort would be crucial to a cartel's success. However, Moscow has not indicated any real interest in establishing such a cartel. In fact, Russia has succeeded on its own in becoming the main supplier to the European market, and it is positioning itself to become the main supplier to Asia. A number of the other leading natural gas exporters—Canada, Australia, and Trinidad and Tobago—are industrialized free-market-oriented states and would most likely not seek the establishment of a cartel. Moreover international gas export markets are just beginning to emerge in some LNG trade, hampering the effectiveness of a global cartel. At the same time, a number of gas producers, such as Egypt and even Iran itself, are courting international investment to develop their LNG ability. Joining a natural gas cartel would hamper their chances of receiving significant foreign investment to develop their LNG industries. Additionally, unlike oil, which is traded on exchanges that constantly updates the market price based on supply and demand, most gas is sold under contracts that allow buyers to lock in prices for as long as 25 years, creating a further difficulty to coordinate actions of a cartel.

Chapter 12
Saudi Arabia

For nearly half a century, Saudi Arabia has been the world's most important oil producer, and through its dominance of the Organization of Petroleum Exporting Countries it has played the leading role in determining global levels of oil exports and, consequently, world oil prices. This leadership role is likely to continue for future decades since the country possesses the world's largest proven oil reserves—a fifth of the global total. Saudi Arabia also enjoys extremely low production costs. Saudi Arabia's key power instrument has been its spare oil production capacity. Riyadh's importance in the oil market has won the Saudi regime strong strategic backing from the United States and an important role in Middle East politics.

Saudi Arabia's and OPEC's position in the world oil market has shifted over time. Significant production in Saudi Arabia and other Arab producers commenced in the 1930s, relatively late compared with the United States, Russia, and other early producers. In the 1970s, OPEC commanded more than 60 percent of world oil production. In contrast, by the beginning of the twenty-first century, non-OPEC production had grown significantly and OPEC production stood at 40 percent of global output. Current OPEC membership includes Algeria, Kuwait, Libya, Nigeria, Qatar, Saudi Arabia, the United Arab Emirates, Iran, Iraq, Indonesia, and Venezuela. The fact that Russia, the world's second-largest oil producer and largest overall energy exporter, is not an OPEC member and does not coordinate its export policies with OPEC has created a huge dent in the power of the oil group.

OPEC was formed in 1960, aiming to offset the control of the major international oil companies in oil production in their countries as well as in distribution. As was noted in Chapter 2, the group made its impact primarily in 1973–74, with the declaration of an oil embargo on the United States, Israel, and the Netherlands following the 1973 Yom Kippur War. The declared embargo did not lead to the suspension of supplies to any states. But because of the already tight conditions of the world market prior to the declaration, it triggered a 400 percent increase in world oil prices within a short period. In contrast to conventional wisdom, however, this price jump was sparked not by the boycott but by the previous decline in spare U.S. oil production. These tight market conditions allowed the OPEC declaration to further boost already rising prices. As we have noted, in periods when oil production significantly outstrips demand, these political declarations and developments have less impact on oil prices.

The declaration of the embargo aided the OPEC states in their previously articulated goal of nationalizing their oil industries. Most of the Middle East producers in OPEC nationalized between 1973 and 1975. Saudi Arabia took a much more gradual approach, completing the nationalization of Aramco in the early 1980s.

Historically, Saudi Arabia has attempted a policy of maintaining long-term moderate oil prices to extend the life of petroleum as a major component of the global economy. Sustained high oil prices drive consumers to seek alternative sources of energy and conservation and can stifle demand through economic impact. At the same time, sustained low oil prices hurt the income base of oil exporters and prevent investment in generating new production. Thus, throughout most of the 1980s and 1990s, Saudi Arabia conducted policies that helped maintain world oil prices in a range of between $22 and $28 per barrel. Maintaining prices in this band demanded a highly skilled foreign policy balancing act to elicit cooperation from both OPEC and non-OPEC producers to produce appropriate levels of oil. After 2005, OPEC dismantled its oil price band and has not instituted a new price policy, perhaps due to a change it its capability.

Saudi Arabia has been able to conduct its price policy due to its spare or "swing capacity." The Saudis have maintained idle oil production capacity that in a short period it can rev up and add to its export volumes in order to moderate world oil prices. This additional capacity has endowed Saudi Arabia with its kingmaker position in the world oil market, but it is quite an expensive and extraordinary tool to maintain. And during the latest round of sustained high oil prices Saudi Arabia has not kicked in its spare capacity and significantly expanded production, leading to speculation that perhaps Saudi Arabia no longer has significant swing capacity. Alternatively, following the ascent to the throne of King Abdullah in 2005, the kingdom may have had a change of heart on the wisdom of attempting to maintain moderate world oil prices, or the new leadership may not be in a position domestically to conduct this policy at this time.

Saudi Arabia's traditional interest in moderate oil prices dovetails with that of the United States. Indeed, Saudi-U.S. relations are the example par excellence of the overlap of oil and diplomacy. Saudi Arabia works hard to maintain its position as a primary oil exporter to the United States. In return, the United States maintains security and military forces in the Persian Gulf and protects the ruling regime. Washington also refrains from any concrete pressure on the ruling regime to conduct democratic reforms or improve its human rights record. To maintain a prime position in the U.S. import market, Aramco sells oil to the United States at a discount to offset transportation costs. This essentially amounts to a subsidy by Saudi Arabia of exports to the United States.[1]

However, Saudi Arabia's close relationship with the United States goes beyond the "oil for security" formula in which the U.S. guarantees the security of the ruling Saud regime in exchange for the regime ensuring the free flow of oil at reasonable prices. Rather, for a large part of the second half of the twentieth century, Washington and Riyadh had a common agenda: battling the Soviet Union and the spread of communism in the Middle East and Third World.[2] Saudi Arabia, for example, played a central role in sponsoring and initiating armed Islamic resistance to the Soviet presence in Afghanistan in the 1980s. However, the demise of the Soviet threat, the Saudi origin of most of the September 11 terrorists, the tepid Saudi response to the terror attacks, and the consequences of the U.S. invasion and presence in Iraq have put huge strains on the Washington-Riyadh relationship. The post-September 11 era in the United States has created an additional constraint on this relationship. Until then, a number of the basic underlying assumptions and understandings between the two countries were confined to the realm of quiet diplomacy and unspoken understandings. Since then, relations between the U.S. and Saudi Arabia have become an object of wide public scrutiny in the United States.[3]

Making OPEC Work

Even though it plays a leading role in OPEC, Riyadh has frequently been at odds with other OPEC members over setting world oil prices. Producers with large populations, such as Iran and Venezuela, which need high oil revenues to maintain public services, have frequently challenged Saudi Arabian pricing policies. Riyadh's spare capacity has served as a means of pressure on producers within OPEC and outside the organization to cooperate with Saudi Arabia on price policies. As noted by energy experts Morse and Richard, "Unlike the nuclear deterrent, the Saudi weapon is actively used when required."[4] Saudi Arabia has in a limited number of instances put into action its spare capacity and drowned the world oil market with production, leading to a sharp decline in prices, in order to pressure these countries to come into line with Riyadh's policies and cut back exports. The most recent instance was in response to a challenge from Venezuela. In the 1990s, Caracas attempted to maximize production and ignored its OPEC output quota. By the winter of 1996–97, Caracas was producing over half a million barrels a day above its quota and had supplanted Saudi Arabia as the major supplier to the United States. In response, Saudi Arabia raised its own production by a million barrels a day, leading to the oil price collapse of 1998. Riyadh paid a high price in revenues through this action, but succeeded in reasserting its leadership of OPEC and even compelling some non-OPEC producers to support its pricing policies.[5]

Saudi Arabia has succeeded in an enormous policy feat in preserving OPEC for so long. The organization is comprised of countries with enormous differences in policies, domestic needs, values, and regime type. Member states include those with both large and small reserves. Morse and Jaffe write that

They have radically different political regimes, ranging from authoritarian to democratic to social democratic republics to Islamic republics to traditional monarchies. Some want high prices, others much lower prices, depending on their reserve levels; some want to cooperate closely with large oil-consuming countries, whereas others prefer confrontation; and some members have even gone to war with one another.[6]

Still, Saudi Arabia seeks stable oil prices not only to prevent American and other consumers from seeking substitutes for oil, but also in order to maintain a stable domestic economy. While many consumers think of the "oil crisis" as taking place in the 1970s following the Middle East Yom Kippur War, for major oil producers like Saudi Arabia the real crisis was the subsequent crash of oil prices in the mid-1980s, when in 1986 prices fell below $10 per barrel. The burden of adjusting to changed oil prices is even more difficult for major exporters than for consumers.

The Saudi economic system is an exemplar rentier state, highly dependent on oil revenues, which make up 70 percent of government revenues (funding a large state sector) and 40 percent of gross domestic product. To be sure, these numbers represent progress since the crash of the 1980s, with the kingdom having made some progress in economic reforms, allowing more room for private enterprise. Yet, Riyadh clearly has not succeeded in significantly diversifying its economy. Nor have state planners devised ways to run the extensive government subsidies and economic ventures in an economically efficient manner.

Moreover, Riyadh does not allow foreign ownership in the oil sector, which constrains plans to expand production even more. In fact, Saudi Arabia's oil production has been flat for close to three decades. During the latest round of sustained high prices, Saudi Arabia has, however, diverted a significant portion of its increased revenues to investments in oil production to improve its long-term results.

Saudi oil policies and production are conducted under the auspices of the national oil company, Saudi Aramco. The company is a direct arm of the ruling family. So is the kingdom itself: the Saudi government does not make any pretense at being democratic, nor does it allow any formal political opposition. Aramco and the ruling family, however, are not immune to domestic constraints and debate. In recent years, opposition members and even citizens close to the regime have demanded greater transparency in production and export data and policies.

The lack of transparency in Aramco's activities means that there are questions about the precise level of Saudi Arabia's oil reserves. This, in turn, creates additional uncertainty about long-term trends in the international oil market. Due to the decline in production of a number of its veteran oil fields, Saudi Arabia needs to increase new production by over 700,000 barrels a day each year just to maintain its production level.

In recent years, oil production infrastructure and foreign workers in the oil industry have been targeted by terrorist groups operating in Saudi Arabia. The regime has also been threatened for a number of decades by Osama bin Laden, who has used, in addition to terror, mass media outlets to challenge the ruling family's oil policies and point to corruption in the regime. These attacks have succeeded in creating a perception of instability of the ruling regime. In addition, they have had a significant impact on international oil prices under the prevailing tight market conditions, even though they have not inflicted any damage on Saudi Arabia's production and export ability.

Nonetheless, it is clear that the kingdom will continue to play a dominant role in the world oil export market. At the same time, significant uncertainties exist about the long-term stability of the ruling regime and Saudi Arabia's ability to retain a swing capacity and thus the ruling's family's ability to maintain the state's unique role in the world economy and political system.

Chapter 13
Conclusion

This examination of the interaction between energy and international politics has clearly demonstrated that the two are integrally interlinked. Commercial and political considerations influence each other and can rarely be neatly separated. An integrated world oil market has increased the degree of interdependence in the world economic and political system. Each state's oil consumption affects the price for all consumers, and small changes in production ability or stability in oil exporting or key transit states affect the global oil market for all. Moreover, all countries face the common threat of global climate change. No country can individually protect itself from the impact of global climate change, and the danger a state confronts is not directly proportional to the extent of its emissions.

Sustained high oil prices in the integrated world market and emerging climate change, while seemingly threatening, may serve an important positive function: as a catalyst to move the world from a hydrocarbon era to a new technological age, especially in the sphere of transportation. Low oil prices and the ease and versatility of petroleum use have kept humanity stuck in the hydrocarbon lifestyle and prevented a technological jump in the sphere of transportation. The prevailing modes of transportation in use today are not significantly different than those that prevailed half a century ago. The threat of climate change and sustained high oil prices may push hydrocarbon man to use his technological capability to invent a new mode of transportation, and to think beyond the car.

In previous decades, academic research on the politics of energy supply focused on the politics of oil. In contrast, this book devotes equivalent attention to the politics of natural gas. This reflects two developments: natural gas represents the fastest-growing fuel in terms of global consumption, and the nature of natural gas transport ties it considerably more to politics between states than most other fuel sources, including, in many cases, oil supply.

In extended discussions of the politics of natural gas supply, *Energy Politics* contends that the establishment of a major supply pipeline between countries is more often an expression of the relations between the countries than a tool to build them. As has been shown, no "peace pipeline" has been built between states, and there are no cases in which linking energy infrastructure has contributed to conflict resolution.

In the cases where pipelines preceded the establishment of cooperative political relations, such as the aftermath of the Soviet breakup, pipelines and transit relations have often served as a source of friction and contention between states. However, the value of these relationships as a model for weighing the pros and cons of various gas supply relationships should not be exaggerated, since the infrastructure inherited in post-empire collapse functions quite differently from that willingly established between two or more states. Moscow's winter energy conflicts with Belarus, Ukraine, and Georgia in 2006 and 2007 spurred Europe and others to reevaluate their energy security relationship and growing dependence on natural gas supplies from Russia's Gazprom. However, while it is important to weigh the wisdom of this dependence, extrapolating from Moscow's relations with the former Soviet republics is not very illuminating. Due to the relative symmetry of dependence between Moscow and Europe, the potential supply vulnerability of Western European states is much lower than that of the former Soviet states, and Russia's dealings with its former Soviet neighbors are not necessarily a model for the pattern of Russia's future gas supplies to Europe.

At the same time, studying Russia's supply relations with its former Soviet neighbors is instructive as to the role of transit states in supply relations. While consumers and suppliers rarely upset natural gas supply relations, transit states are more frequently tempted to use this lever of influence. Accordingly, gas supply relations that involve transit states require a much higher degree of management and are inherently less stable than direct natural gas supply relations. Economic gains for transit states are meager and often overestimated by those attempting to understand what a state stands to gain by serving as such. Still, the political gains can be meaningful when they succeed in carving out a regional or international role as major energy transit states.

The most important determinant of the stability of a natural gas supply relationship is the degree of symmetry of dependence. If the supplier needs the market as much as the consumer does, in the long run stable supply relations will prevail. This has been seen for Moscow's gas supply relations with Europe over three decades. But there is a caveat to this claim: there may be a difference in the short and long run. In the long run, symmetry in dependence can almost guarantee stable supplies; in the short run supplies can be withheld in crisis periods, and this can have a more catastrophic impact on the consumer than on the supplier—unless the consumer maintains adequate energy stocks in storage. Energy storage is one of the most useful techniques to reduce the dangers of supply disruptions. Despite that, most states do not maintain adequate storage supplies because of the high costs (which require taxpayers to pay for a service that may be useful only in extraordinary situations).

As we have discussed, natural gas supply relations are highly influenced by and affect the politics between the linked states. In contrast, oil supply flows are becoming less and less political. Geographic proximity more than geopolitical propinquity chiefly determines the directions of oil supply flows today. South American producers deliver nearly all their oil exports to the United States, Russia and the Caspian states deliver most of their oil to Europe and Mediterranean countries, and the Middle East supplies oil chiefly to the states of Asia. Despite the fact that it serves as the security guard of most of the oil-producing states in the Persian Gulf, the United States imports significantly less oil from the region than does Europe in both absolute and relative terms. Moreover, President Hugo Chávez's vocal campaign against Washington has not led to any reduction in deliveries of Venezuela's oil to the United States, which remains Caracas's major export market.

Anticipated Coalitions and Energy Linkages

Energy supply pipelines can provide the means to strengthen geopolitical alliances, as in the case of the Baku-Tbilisi-Ceyhan pipeline, which the involved parties hope will enable Azerbaijan and Georgia to join Euro-Atlantic security structures. However, as stated above, energy infrastructure does not create geopolitical alliances; instead, it tends to reflect them. Most of the pipelines that cross Eurasia were developed during the Soviet period and reflect the realities of that era. In Asia, there are still few pipeline links between states and none between Russia and Asian consumers. If they should be established, they would represent increased cooperation within Asia and greater Russian integration into Asia. The lack of linkage of Iran into any major export infrastructure projects reflects its strategic isolation.

While much as been made over the potential geopolitical conflict between China and the United States for control of oil supplies, the arguments presented here depict a much more nuanced view. China's rise will certainly entail regional and global adjustments to accommodate its enhanced power, and there are a variety of factors that may lead Washington and Beijing to perceive each other as threatening, but the scramble for the control of oil sources should not be one of the major factors. As presented in *Energy Politics*, legal possession of an oil production site is only a small link in the chain of bringing oil imports home. The larger picture of cooperation or conflict in the world's sea lanes is much more important in determining the extent of threat the sides may present to each other—and currently there are no signs of China challenging Washington's dominance at sea. In fact, at this point, China's increased oil imports increase Beijing's dependence on Washington's policing of the world's sea-lanes. While Chinese oil companies may present a challenge to the dominance of U.S. oil majors in the world oil market, their activities do not snatch control of oil from other producers, but generally increase the total volume of oil produced.

While the United States and Beijing are not in direct competition for control of oil volumes around the globe, Europe and China may in future decades compete for Russian natural gas supplies if a major gas supply pipeline is established between Russia and China. Under these circumstances, Moscow will be in a position to play two major markets against each other, and thus improve its bargaining position vis-à-vis both of them.

A Future Research Agenda

As we noted at the beginning of this study, despite the centrality of energy in the relations between states and in the international political system, only a small percentage of the research published in mainstream journals of political science and international relations deals with energy and politics. The bulk of the publications on the issue are found in policy-oriented and regional studies journals, as indicated by the lion's share of references to academic works in this book. The discipline of international relations was originally anchored in the study of geographic factors: geographic elements of military power, geographic factors in warfare, and conflicts over control over natural resources. Beginning in World War II, abstract concepts of identity and ideology appeared as important factors for study. These rose to prominence following the breakup of the Soviet Union and Yugoslavia at the end of the twentieth century: the subsequent ethnic wars in these two countries seemed to justify the approach that emphasizes the potency of identity and other nonphysical factors in political outcomes.

The study of energy in international relations represents a return to the study of the "geo" of geopolitics. In an integrated world economy, the place of energy is very different from the one it held during the mercantile era, when states scrambled to gain control of oil sources. Yet, as stated throughout this book, energy and politics are highly influenced by each other, and clearly energy security is an element of any state's national security and for most an integral part of their foreign policy.

Among the topics warranting future study in the interaction between energy and politics are the security and political cooperation that has been produced by the emergence of multiple state projects, especially with landlocked states at their core; the mutual impact of natural gas supply on relations between states; the impact of international oil oligarchs on world politics; the effect of liquid natural gas on energy security; the impact of energy infrastructure on war and peace; and the connection between oil and gas production and the emergence of conflict. As discussed in the chapter on conflict, the link between oil and gas and propensity to conflict is still unclear. Quantitative studies have not been able to find a robust link that is not affected by slight changes in the composition of the data set. In addition, in the quantitative studies that show a link between conflict and the presence of oil or natural gas exports, there still is not consensus as to why the link exists.

An additional topic for study is appropriate policy formats to stimulate innovation in the sphere of energy. Governments need to provide incentives that will foster development of new sources of energy and energy-use conservation measures, and to do so without determining themselves what those measures should be.

It is puzzling that, despite the uncontested impact of energy on almost every sphere of human life and the continued sustainability of the planet earth, only a few research and degree programs at major universities focus on the nontechnological aspects of energy. Moreover, few major survey courses in international relations and political science programs dedicate significant class hours to the topic of energy and politics. Part of the explanation for this puzzle seems to lie in the inherent interdisciplinary nature of the study of energy, which requires a synthesis of economics, politics, law, geology, environmental studies, and technological topics. The emergence of new interdisciplinary energy studies programs will contribute to the formation of energy policy-making as well to our academic understanding of the impact of energy on society, security, and politics.

Policy Implications

As oil prices began to reach and maintain new highs beginning in 2003, energy security gained ground as a major national security and foreign policy issue around the globe. This response is similar to that when high oil prices prevailed in the 1970s. However, in the periods of low oil prices in between, states tended to reduce the attention and resources they expended on energy security, and as a concern it was demoted to the lower levels of the policy ladder. Countries tend to undertake energy security-enhancing measures under conditions of urgency, and only when prices are highest do they begin to acquire additional supplies and infrastructure. It would be preferable to address energy security needs more intensely during periods when oil supplies are copious and prices low.

The spread of democracy has been one of the major features of the world political system during the last quarter of the twentieth century. In 1975, only 30 states had popularly elected governments; in 2005 that number had soared almost four times to 119. However, the major oil exporters among them have begun to slip backward on the path toward democracy, and few of the veteran oil-producing states show signs of transitioning to democracy. As seen in *Energy Politics,* the revenue accrued by governments in major oil and natural gas exporters renders transitions to democracy particularly difficult. Accordingly, mainstream policy prescriptions for promoting democratic transitions are not applicable to oil-exporting states. A new body of literature needs to be developed to address the unique challenge of creating the conditions for the democratic transition of major energy exporters. In addition, the United States and other countries that are attempting to promote democratic transitions in the Middle East and beyond must accept that in their current form, these policy prescriptions are futile, and will have little impact on the major energy exporters in the region.

World economic institutions, such as the World Bank and the International Monetary Fund, need to take a new look at the use of oil and gas exports as a means to aid developing countries. As we have discussed, in the current economic system, states that export natural resources tend to fare worse economically than resource-poor states. Major oil exporters tend to develop undiversified and unstable economies that are vulnerable to the ebbs and flows of world oil prices, with large-scale unemployment and underemployment. Despite this trend, international financial institutions like the World Bank and the International Monetary Fund continue to promote oil and natural gas export as a source of revenue to help alleviate poverty in developing countries. This was seen in the case of Chad, where the World Bank took an unprecedented role as a financier, financial recruiter, and director of the revenue use framework to attempt to use Chad's oil wealth to alleviate poverty. As of late 2008, these efforts do not seem to have produced results, and Chad appears to be falling into the same economic and institutional pattern as other oil producers in the developing world.

We began *Energy Politics* by noting that there is a global energy divide when it comes to access to regular electric power. Close to a third of the world's population do not have electricity. Consequently, the lifestyle of this third of the planet is very different from that of the other two-thirds when it comes to health and development issues. Addressing the global energy divide will be a major challenge in coming decades and will most likely serve as a major item on the agenda of the world's major financial and development institutions. Addressing the energy divide may also become an important domestic political issue in a number of developing countries, such as India and China. The demand to provide regular electricity access to the third of the planet's residents that are currently without it will also place additional pressure on how to deal with the threat of climate change.

In the current state of energy and politics, two reverse trends are taking place concurrently: states are privatizing and unbundling their energy sectors and allowing market forces to greatly affect their actual energy policies, while at the same time the challenges of energy security are demanding complicated and long-term policy responses. This policy runs major risks. It is by no means clear that market forces can achieve all three elements of energy security: reliability of supply, affordability, and friendliness to the environment. At this point, few states have devised market mechanisms that produce energy policies that are friendly to the environment or that take into consideration the needs of future generations. Market forces will not take care of energy for all. In addition, market forces do not create the expensive redundancies in supply sources and types that reduce consumer vulnerability.

We should rethink the retreat of the state from the energy sector. Just as market forces cannot provide for national security at a level that most citizens around the globe demand, the market cannot provide adequate energy security. Certainly, protecting the environment will not be provided for by market forces. The needs of future generations and sustainability of the planet may also require the state to intervene on their behalf. The state needs to be involved when it comes to the question of energy and politics.

Notes

Introduction

1. "Cross-Border Oil and Gas Pipelines: Problems and Prospects," ESMAP (2003) (Washington, D.C.: UNDP/World Bank Energy Sector Management Assistance Program, 2003), 45.

2. Quoted in Friedemann Mueller, "Energy Security: Demands Imposed on German and European Foreign Policy by a Changed Configuration in the World Energy Market," SWP Research Paper, German Institute for International and Security Affairs (Stiftung Wissenschaft und Politik), RP 2, English version of SWP-Studie 33/06 (Berlin, January 2007), 5.

3. Dick Cheney, keynote speech in Vilnius, Lithuania, May 4, 2006.

4. Daniel Yergin, *The Prize: The Epic Quest for Oil, Money and Power* (New York: Free Press, 1992), 171.

5. The "Seven Sisters" refers to Jersey (Exxon), Socony-Vacuum (Mobil), Standard of California (Chevron), and Texaco, in addition to Gulf, Royal Dutch/Shell, and British Petroleum. See Yergin, *The Prize*, 503.

6. *Key World Energy Statistics 2005* (Vienna: IEA, 2005), 10.

7. Yergin, *The Prize*, 718. This trend of fuel efficiency, however, was reversed in recent years in the United States. In addition, Americans have at least until 2008 been driving larger vehicles longer distances. Thus, since 1990, the number of gallons consumed on a per vehicle basis has risen substantially. See Austan Goolsbee, "A Country Less Dependent on Oil Is Free to Make Other New Year's Resolutions," *New York Times*, January 4, 2007.

8. *Key World Energy Statistics*, 6, 33.

9. *Forbes* magazine's annual list of billionaires includes each year a significant number of individuals who accumulated their wealth from oil, natural gas, and mineral ownership. In Russia, for instance, *Forbes* identified more than 36 oligarchs of mineral wealth as billionaires. See Marshall I. Goldman, "Putin and the Oligarchs," *Foreign Affairs* (November/December 2004): 33.

10. See *The Future of Coal: Options for a Carbon Constrained World* (Cambridge, Mass.: MIT Press, 2007).

11. International Energy Agency, *World Energy Outlook 2002* (Paris: IEA, 2002).

12. John P. Holdren and Kirk R. Smith, "Energy, the Environment, and Health," chapter 3 in *World Energy Assessment: Energy and the Challenge of Sustainability*, ed. José Goldemberg (New York: UNDP, 2000), 68.

13. Carl Walske, "Nuclear Electric Power and the Proliferation of Nuclear Weapon States," *International Security* 1, no. 3 (Winter 1977): 94–106; Robert L.

Paarlberg, "Food, Oil, and Coercive Resource Power," *International Security* 3, no. 2 (Autumn 1978): 3–19; Richard R. Fagen, "Mexican Petroleum and U.S. National Security," *International Security* 4, no. 1 (Summer 1979): 39–53; Ray Dafter, "World Oil Production and Security of Supplies," *International Security* 4, no. 3 (Winter 1979–1980): 154–76; David A. Deese, "Energy: Economics, Politics, and Security," *International Security* 4, no. 3 (Winter 1979–1980): 140–53; Thane Gustafson, "Energy and the Soviet Bloc," *International Security* 6, no. 3 (Winter 1981–1982): 65–89; Robert J. Lieber, "Energy, Economics, and Security in Alliance Perspective," *International Security* 4, no. 4 (Spring 1980): 139–63; Robert J. Lieber, "Oil and Power After the Gulf War," *International Security* 17, no. 1 (Summer 1992): 155–76.

14. Sean M. Lynn-Jones and Steven Miller, eds., *Global Dangers: Changing Dimensions of International Security* (Cambridge, Mass.: MIT Press, 1995).

15. Among the most noteworthy, M. A. Adelman, *The Genie Out of the Bottle: World Oil Since 1970* (Cambridge, Mass.: MIT Press, 1996).

16. Joseph Nye and David Deese, eds., *Energy and Security* (Cambridge, Mass.: Ballinger, 1981).

17. Roy Licklider, "The Power of Oil: The Arab Oil Weapon and the Netherlands, the United Kingdom, Canada, Japan, and the United States," *International Studies Quarterly* 32, no. 2 (June 1988): 205–26; R. James Woolsey, "Defeating the Oil Weapon," *Commentary* 114, no. 2 (September 2002): 29–33.

18. Joseph S. Nye, "Balancing Nonproliferation and Energy Security," *Technology Review* (December 1978/January 1979): 48–57; Carl Walske, "Nuclear Electric Power and the Proliferation of Nuclear Weapon States," *International Security* 1, no. 3 (Winter 1977): 94–106.

19. Examples include Louis Turner, "The Oil Majors in World Politics," *International Affairs* 52, no. 3 (July 1976): 368–80; Louis Turner, *Oil Companies in the International System* (London: Royal Institute of International Affairs, 1978); 2nd ed. (Winchester, Mass.: Allen & Unwin, 1980); Karl Kaiser, "Transnational Relations as a Threat to Democratic Process," *International Organization* 25, no. 3 (Summer 1971); Joseph S. Nye, Jr., and Robert O. Keohane, "Transnational Relations and World Politics: An Introduction," *International Organization* 25, no. 3 (Summer 1971).

20. Steve Chan, "The Consequences of Expensive Oil on Arms Transfers," *Journal of Peace Research*, 17, no. 3 (1980): 235–46; Lewis W. Snider, "Arms Exports for Oil Imports? The Test of a Nonlinear Model," *Journal of Conflict Resolution* 28, no. 4 (December 1984): 665–700; Robert J. Lieber, "Oil and Power After the Gulf War," *International Security* 17, no. 1 (Summer 1992): 155–76; Marc A. Levy, "Is the Environment a National Security Issue?" *International Security* 20, no. 2 (Autumn 1995): 35–62.

21. John G. Ikenberry, "The Irony of State Strength: Comparative Responses to the Oil Shocks in the 1970s," *International Organization* 40, no. 1 (Winter 1986): 105–37.

22. Robert O. Keohane, "The International Energy Agency: State Influence and Transgovernmental Politics," *International Organization* 32, no. 4 (Autumn 1978): 929–51.

23. See Chapter 2 for extensive examination of this topic. See also Ben Smith, "Oil Wealth and Regime Survival in the Developing World, 1960–1999," *APSR* 48, no. 2 (2004): 232–46; Richard M. Auty, *Resource Abundance and Economic Development* (Oxford: Oxford University Press, 2001); Svetlana Tsalik, ed., *Caspian Oil Windfalls: Who Will Benefit?* (New York: Open Society Institute, 2003).

24. See Chapter 5 for an extensive review of the literature on the impact of oil on inter- and intrastate conflict.

Chapter 1. Energy and Regime Type

1. The IMF statistical analysis terms the major energy producers the IMF fuel exporters analytical group, with the criteria that over the past five years, the average share of fuel exports exceeds 40 percent of total exports and the average value of fuel exports exceeds $500 million.

2. Jeffrey D. Sachs and Andrew M. Warner, "Natural Resource Abundance and Economic Growth," NBER Working Paper 5398 (Cambridge, Mass.: National Bureau of Economic Research, 1995).

3. Terry Lynn Karl, *The Paradox of Plenty: Oil Booms and Petro-States* (Berkeley: University of California Press, 1997); Karl, "The Perils of the Petro-State: Reflections on the Paradox of Plenty," *Journal of International Affairs* 53, no. 1 (Fall 1999): 31–48.

4. Karl, "The Perils of the Petro-State," 37.

5. Mohsen Fardmanesh, "Dutch Disease Economics and the Oil Syndrome: An Empirical Study," *World Development* 19, no. 6 (1991).

6. John Wakeman-Linn et al., *Managing Oil Wealth: The Case of Azerbaijan* (Washington, D.C.: IMF, 2004), 1.

7. Jahangir Amuzegar, *Managing the Oil Wealth: OPEC's Windfalls and Pitfalls* (London: I.B. Tauris, 1999), 10.

8. Giacomo Luciani, "Resources, Revenues, and Authoritarianism in the Arab World," in *Political Liberalization and Democratization in the Arab World*, ed. Rex Brynen, Bahdat Korany, and Paul Noble, vol. 1, *Theoretical Perspectives* (Boulder, Colo.: Lynne Rienner, 1995), 215.

9. See http://www.imf.org/external/pubs/ft/weo/2006/01/pdf/c2.pdf.

10. Amuzegar, *Managing the Oil Wealth*, 208.

11. Ugo Fasano, "Review of the Experience with Oil Stabilization and Savings Funds in Selected Countries," IMF Working Paper 11/112 (Washington, D.C.: International Monetary Fund, 2000), quoted in Wakeman-Linn et al., *Managing Oil Wealth*, 5.

12. See, for instance, "Addressing the Resource Curse," in Philippe Le Billon, *Fuelling War: Natural Resources and Armed Conflict*, Adelphi Paper 373 (London: International Institute for Strategic Studies, 2005), 51–79.

13. For expanded discussion of the Chad-Cameroon pipeline project, see Chapter 3.

14. This has been coined the "Third Wave" of democracy by Samuel Huntington; see Huntington, *The Third Wave: Democratization in the Late Twentieth Century* (Norman: University of Oklahoma Press, 1991).

15. According to Hazem Beblawi, "The Rentier State in the Arab World," in *The Rentier State*, ed. Hazem Beblawi and Giacomo Luciani (New York: Croom Helm with Methuen, 1987), 51.

16. Beblawi, "The Rentier State," 52.

17. Giacomo Luciani, "Allocation vs. Production States: A Theoretical Framework," in *The Arab State*, ed. Giacomo Luciani (London: Routledge, 1990).

18. Theda Skocpol, "Rentier State and Shi'a Islam in the Iranian Revolution," *Theory and Society* 11, no. 3 (May 1982): 269.

19. Kamal Nazer Yasin, "Huge State Spending Increase in Iran Driven by President's Political Agenda," *Eurasia Insight* 8 (March 2006).

20. Michael L. Ross, "Does Oil Hinder Democracy?" *World Politics* 53, no. 3 (2001): 325–61.

21. For an important analysis of a semi-rentier state, see Rex Brynen, "Economic Crisis and Post-Rentier Democratization in the Arab World: The Case of Jordan," *Canadian Journal of Political Science* 25, no. 1 (March 1992): 69–97.

22. Benjamin Smith, "Oil Wealth and Regime Survival in the Developing World, 1960–1999," *American Journal of Political Science* 48, no. 2 (April 2004): 232–46.

23. Skocpol, "Rentier State," 280.

Chapter 2. Foreign Policy

1. Richard Lugar, speech at NATO summit in Riga, Latvia, November 28–29, 2006.

2. *New York Times,* January 5, 2006.

3. For an excellent discussion on resource nationalism, see Edward L. Morse, "Oil Policies and Resource Nationalism," *Geopolitics of Energy* 27, no. 4 (April 2005): 6–9.

4. Quoted in Javier Blas and Carola Hoyos, "Oil Wrestling: How Nationalist Politics Has Muscled Back into World Energy," *Financial Times,* May 5, 2006.

5. Quoted in Blas and Hoyos, "Oil Wrestling."

6. "Chávez Offers Cheap Oil to Allies," Agence France-Presse, April 30, 2007.

7. "Plan for South American Pipeline Has Ambitions Beyond Gas," *New York Times,* December 2, 2006.

8. Simon Romero, "Oil Discord Stirs Venezuelan Angst," *International Herald Tribune,* July 25, 2007, 11.

9. For example, "Putin Denies Using Energy as a Weapon," *Financial Times,* February 1, 2007, 1; A. F. Alhajji, "The Oil Weapon: Past, Present, and Future," *Oil and Gas Journal* 103, no. 17 (May 2, 2005): 22–30; R. James Woolsey, "Defeating the Oil Weapon," *Commentary* 114, no. 2 (September 2002): 29–33.

10. M. A. Adelman, "Oil Fallacies," *Foreign Policy* (Spring 1991): 14.

11. The energy-intensive economies of China and India are much more vulnerable to price surges.

12. A. F. Alhajji, "The Oil Weapon: Past, Present and Future," *Oil and Gas Journal* 103, no. 17 (May 2, 2005).

13. Carola Hoyos, "Oil Weapon That Rocked World's Economy," *Financial Times,* October 2003, 1.

14. Hoyos, "Oil Weapon," 1.

15. Gazprom is an exception. Its contracts with the former Soviet republics are generally set on a yearly basis.

16. Friedemann Mueller, "Energy Security: Demands Imposed on German and European Foreign Policy by a Changed Configuration in the World Energy Market," SWP Research Paper, German Institute for International and Security Affairs (Stiftung Wissenschaft und Politik), RP 2 (English version of SWP-Studie 33/06, January 2007, Berlin), 15.

17. Quoted in "Poland Intends to Cut Reliance on Russian Gas," *International Herald Tribune,* November 18, 2005, 13.

18. Quoted at NATO summit in Bucharest, APA news service, April 3, 2008.

19. "Energeticheskaya strategiya Rossii na period do 2020 goda" (Energy Strategy of Russia to the Year 2020), Government of the Russian Federation Decree 1234-r, August 28, 2003.

20. During the February 2008 natural gas supply crisis between Russia and Ukraine, the two sides decided to remove this intermediary, which seemed to be incurring higher costs to Ukraine and cutting into Moscow's profits.

21. "Gazprom Threat to Supplies," *Financial Times*, April 20, 2006.

Chapter 3. Pipeline Trends and International Politics

1. "World Oil Transit Chokepoints," Energy Information Administration, U.S. Department of Energy, November 2005; http://www.eia.doe.gov/emeu/cabs/World_Oil_Transit_Chokepoints/Background.html.

2. President Nursultan Nazarbayev, quoted in *Kazakhstan News Bulletin* 5, no. 54 (December 21, 2005).

3. President Ilham Aliyev, Bled, Slovenia, August 27, 2006 (author recorded statement).

4. H. E. Karim Massimov, address at University of Haifa, October 31, 2006.

5. *New York Times*, January 8, 2006.

6. For more on the Baku-Tbilisi-Ceyhan project and the implications for international relations, see Brenda Shaffer, "From Pipedream to Pipeline: Lessons from the Baku-Tbilisi-Ceyhan Pipeline Project," *Current History* (October 2005): 343–47.

7. Akram Esanov, Martin Raiser, and Willem Buiter, "Nature's Blessing or Nature's Curse," in *Energy, Wealth and Governance in the Caucasus and Central Asia*, ed. Richard M. Auty and Indra de Soysa (New York: Routledge, 2006), 41.

8. Post-Soviet Azerbaijan was born into a war with neighboring Armenia centered on control of the Nagorno-Karabagh region. The state of war between the two countries and the unresolved border between them precludes transit options through Armenia.

9. Author's interview with Vafa Quluzade, chief foreign policy advisor to President Heydar Aliyev, April 2005, Baku. April 2005, Baku.

10. Author's interview with Vafa Quluzade, and additional interviews by the author with political advisers and staff members of Azerbaijan's President Heydar Aliyev, conducted in spring 2005, Baku.

11. Bill Richardson, quoted in Stephen Kinzer, "On Piping Out Caspian Oil, U.S. Insists That Cheaper, Shorter Way, Isn't Better," *New York Times*, November 8, 1998.

12. Robert Ebel, "A Pipeline That May End as a Pipe Dream," interview with Andy Clark, *Newsliner* (November 19, 1999); Ebel: "Pipelines are supposed to be built for commercial reasons, not political reasons," quoted in Kinzer, "On Piping Caspian Oil."

13. Quoted in Kinzer, "On Piping Caspian Oil."

14. Author's interview with Vafa Quluzade. For more on Iranian-Azerbaijan relations, see Brenda Shaffer, "The Islamic Republic of Iran—Is It Really?" in *Limits of Culture: Islam and Foreign Policy*, ed. Brenda Shaffer (Cambridge, Mass.: MIT Press, 2006).

15. Based on author's interview with a political adviser to President Heydar Aliyev, March 2003, Baku.

16. For an excellent discussion of the Armenian American lobby's efforts,

see David King and Miles Pomper, "Congress, Constituencies and U.S. Foreign Policy in the Caspian," in Shaffer, ed. *Limits of Culture*, 167–92.

17. Charles McPherson, senior adviser in the Oil, Gas, Mining, and Chemicals Department of the World Bank, in "Government, Transparency, and Sustainable Development," in *Energy and Security: Toward a New Foreign Policy Strategy*, ed. Jan H. Kalicki and David L. Goldwyn (Baltimore: Johns Hopkins University Press, 2005), 480–81.

18. Philippe Le Billon, *Fueling War: Natural Resources and Armed Conflict*, Adelphi Paper 373 (London: International Institute for Strategic Studies, 2005), 67.

19. The license has subsequently been extended.

20. Donald R. Norland, "Innovations of the Chad/Cameroon Pipeline Project: Thinking Outside the Box," *Mediterranean Quarterly* 14, no. 2 (2003): 2.

21. The statement can be found at http://go.worldbank.org/WAN I8L6AO0.

22. Paul Raebern, "Commentary: This Clean Oil Project Is Tainted Already," *Business Week* (April 9, 2001).

23. Quoted by BBC News, January 13, 2006.

24. Scott Pegg, "Can Policy Intervention Beat the Resource Curse? Evidence from the Chad-Cameroon Pipeline Project," *African Affairs* 105, no. 418 (2006): 22.

Chapter 4. Conflict

1. Caroline Daniel, "Kissinger Warns of Energy Conflict," *Financial Times*, June 2, 2005.

2. Richard Lugar, speech at NATO Summit, Riga, Latvia, November 28–29, 2006.

3. Michael T. Klare, *Resource Wars: The New Landscape of Global Conflict* (New York: Metropolitan Books, 2001), 28. See also Klare, *Rising Powers, Shrinking Planet: The New Geopolitics of Energy* (New York: Metropolitan Books, 2008) and Klare, *Blood and Oil: The Dangers and Consequences of America's Growing Dependency on Imported Petroleum* (New York: Metropolitan Books, 2004).

4. Robert A. Manning, *The Asian Energy Factor* (New York: Palgrave, 2000), 191.

5. Rainer Lagoni, "Oil and Gas Deposits Across National Frontiers," *American Journal of International Law* 73, no. 2 (April 1979): 215–16.

6. Lagoni, "Oil and Gas Deposits," 217.

7. Kohei Hashimoto, Jareer Elass, and Stacy Eller, "Liquefied Natural Gas from Qatar: The Qatargas Project," Geopolitics of Gas Working Paper Series, James A. Baker III Institute for Public Policy Energy Forum, Rice University, December 2004, 12.

8. John J. Maresca, "A 'Peace Pipeline' to End the Nagorno-Karabakh Conflict," *Caspian Crossroads*, no. 1 (Winter 1995).

9. Maresca, "A 'Peace Pipeline.' "

10. See Abbas Maleki and Kaveh Afrasiabi, "Saving the Peace Pipeline," Agence Global, August 16, 2007; Abbas Maleki, "Iran-Pakistan-India Pipeline: Is It a Peace Pipeline?" *Audit of Conventional Wisdom* 7, no. 16 (September 2007).

11. Author's interviews with Indian energy officials, December 2005.

12. Mark H. Hayes and David G. Victor, "Politics, Markets, and the Shift to Gas," in *Natural Gas and Geopolitics: From 1970 to 2040*, ed. David G. Victor, Amy

M. Jaffe, and Mark H. Hayes (New York: Cambridge University Press, 2006), 346–47.

13. Among the extensive literature on the topic, see Macartan Humphreys, "Natural Resources, Conflict, and Conflict Resolution: Uncovering the Mechanisms," *Journal of Conflict Resolution* 49, no. 4 (2005): 508–37; Pierre Englebert and James Ron, "Primary Commodities and War: Congo-Brazzaville's Ambivalent Resource Curse," *Comparative Politics* 37, no. 1 (2004); Paul Collier and Anke Hoeffler, "Greed and Grievance in Civil Wars," Working Paper WPS 2000–18, World Bank, 2000; James D. Fearon, "Primary Commodity Export and Civil War," *Journal of Conflict Resolution* 49, no. 4 (August 2005); Karen Ballentine and Jake Sherman, *Beyond Greed and Grievance: The Political Economy of Armed Conflict* (Boulder, Colo.: Lynne Rienner, 2003); James D. Fearon and David D. Laitin, "Ethnicity, Insurgency, and Civil War," *American Political Science Review* 97, no. 1 (2003): 75–90; Phillip Le Billon, "The Political Ecology of War: Natural Resources and Armed Conflict," *Political Geography* 20 (2001): 561–84; Le Billon, *Fueling War: Natural Resources and Armed Conflict,* Adelphi Paper 373 (London: International Institute for Strategic Studies, 2005); Michael Ross, "How Does Natural Resource Wealth Influence Civil War? Evidence from 13 Cases," *International Organization* 58, no. 1 (2004); Indra DeSoysa, "The Resource Curse: Are Civil Wars Driven by Rapacity or Paucity," in *Greed and Grievance: Economic Agendas in Civil Wars,* ed. Mats Berdal and David Malone (Boulder, Colo.: Lynne Rienner, 2003), 113–35.

14. Collier and Hoeffler, "Greed and Grievance in Civil Wars"; also Ian Bannon and Paul Collier, "Natural Resources and Conflict: What We Can Do," in *Natural Resources and Violent Conflict: Options and Actions,* ed. Ian Bannon and Paul Collier (Washington, D.C.: World Bank, 2003), 1–16.

15. See Fearon, "Primary Commodity Export," 500–503, for the claim that oil and gas do not act like other primary commodities in the effect they have on conflict outbreak.

16. For a comprehensive review of the major international relations and political science literature on the link between oil and gas and other natural resources and violent intrastate conflict, see Michael L. Ross, "What Do We Know About Natural Resources and Civil War," *Journal of Peace Research* 41, no. 3 (2004): 337–56; and Humphreys, "Natural Resources."

17. Paul Collier and Anke Hoeffler, *Greed and Grievance in Civil War,* Oxford Economic Papers 56, no. 4 (Oxford: Dept. of Economics, CSAE, 2000), 563–96, Fearon and Laitin, 'Ethnicity, Insurgency, and Civil War."

18. Fearon, "Primary Commodity Export," refutes the findings in the earlier works by Collier and Hoeffler. Fearon states that when the data in Collier and Hoeffler were analyzed on a yearly basis, not grouped by five years, the statistical connection between natural resource commodities and conflict outbreak disappeared.

19. Michael Ross, "A Closer Look at Oil, Diamonds, and Civil War," *Annual Review of Political Science* 9 (2006): 296.

20. Fearon, "Primary Commodity Export," 504; Humphreys wrote that "econometric tests of the effects of natural resources on conflicts, including those presented here, continue to suffer from severe problems of data, model specification, and in particular a sensitivity of coefficient estimates to variations in model specification." See Humphreys, "Natural Resources," 533.

21. Mary Kaldor, Terry Lynn Karl, and Yahia Said, "Introduction," in *Oil Wars,* ed. Mary Kaldor, Terry Lynn Karl, and Yahia Said (London: Pluto Press, 2007), 11.

22. Fearon, "Primary Commodity Exports," 487.

23. Fearon and Laitin, "Ethnicity, Insurgency, and Civil War."

24. Bannon and Collier, "Natural Resources and Conflict," 4.

25. Ross, "How Does Natural Resource Wealth Influence Civil War?"

26. Humphreys, "Natural Resources," 511.

27. Michael L. Ross, "Does Oil Hinder Democracy?" *World Politics* 53, no. 3 (2001): 325–61.

28. Kaldor, Karl, and Said, "Introduction," 24.

29. Ross, "Does Oil Hinder Democracy?"

30. Le Billion, *Fueling War*, 39.

31. Michael Ross, "The Natural Resource Curse," in Bannon and Collier, eds., *Natural Resources and Violent Conflict*, 27, 28.

32. Douglas Birch, "Russia Presses Claim on Arctic," *Boston Globe*, August 2, 2007, 16.

33. *Rossisskaya Gazeta*, August 3, 2007; quoted in *RFE/RL Newsline* 11, no. 145, part I (August 8, 2007).

34. C. J. Chivers, "Eyeing Future Wealth, Russians Plant the Flag on the Arctic Seabed, Below the Polar Cap," *New York Times*, August 3, 2007, 8.

35. Quoted by *RFE/RL Newsline* 11, no. 143, part I (August 6, 2007).

36. "Russia Presses Claim," 16.

37. Interfax News Agency (Moscow), August 1, 2007.

38. Interfax News Agency, June 21, 2007.

39. Chivers, "Eyeing Future Wealth," 8.

40. Quoted by *RFE/RL Newsline* 11, no. 143, part I (August 6, 2007).

41. Kamyar Mehdiyoun, "Ownership of Oil and Gas Resources in the Caspian Sea," *American Journal of International Law* 94, no. 1 (January 2000): 179.

42. Ben N. Dunlap, "Divide and Conquer? The Russian Plan for Ownership of the Caspian Sea," *Boston College International and Comparative Law Review* 27, no. 115 (2004): 120.

43. For more on the Azerbaijani ethnic question in relations between Iran and Azerbaijan, see Brenda Shaffer, *Borders and Brethren: Iran and the Challenge of Azerbaijani Identity* (Cambridge, Mass.: MIT Press, 2002).

44. Author's interview with senior Kazakhstani official, spring 2002.

45. For more on China's energy consumption and energy security policies, see the China case study in Chapter 10.

46. See, for example, Amy Myers Jaffe and Kenneth B. Medlock, III, "China and Northeast Asia," in *Energy and Security: Toward a New Foreign Policy Strategy*, ed. Jan H. Kalicki and David L. Goldwyn (Baltimore: Johns Hopkins University Press, 2005), 268; Kent E. Calder, *Asia's Deadly Triangle* (London: Nicholas Brealy, 1997); Gal Luft, "U.S., China Are on a Collision Course over Oil," *Los Angeles Times*, February 2, 2005; David Zweig and Bi Jianhai, "China's Global Hunt for Energy," *Foreign Affairs* 84, no. 5 (2005): 25–38; Thomas M. Kane and Lawrence W. Serewicz, "China's Hunger: The Consequences of a Rising Demand for Food and Energy," *Parameters* 31 (Autumn 2001): 63–75.

47. See Calder, *Asia's Deadly Triangle*.

48. Zweig and Bi, "China's Global Hunt," 25.

49. See, for example, Amy Myers Jaffe and Steven W. Lewis, "Beijing's Oil Diplomacy," *Survival* 44, no. 1 (Spring 2002): 115–34; Flynt Leverett and Jeffrey Bader, "Managing China-U.S. Energy Competition in the Middle East," *Washington Quarterly* 29, no. 1 (Winter 2005–2006): 187–201; Zweig and Bi, "China's Global Hunt."

50. Leverett and Bader, "Managing China-U.S. Energy Competition," 187.

51. Quoted in *Oil and Gas Journal* (May 1, 2006): 28.

52. Jaffe and Medlock, "China and Northeast Asia," 268.

53. Author's interview with representatives of major Western oil companies invested in Kazakhstan, Almati, Kazakhstan, 2004.

54. Philip Andrews-Speed, Xuanli Liao, and Roland Dannreuther, *The Strategic Implications of China's Energy Needs*, Adelphi Paper 346 (Oxford: Oxford University Press, 2002), 52.

55. Quoted in Xu Yi-chong, "China's Energy Security," *Australian Journal of International Affairs* 60, no. 2 (2006): 278.

56. "China's Energy Conditions and Policies," *People's Daily Online*, December 26, 2007.

Chapter 5. Security

1. Riga Summit Declaration, issued by the heads of state and government participating in the North Atlantic Council meeting in Riga, Latvia, November 29, 2006.

2. Edward L. Morse, "The New Political Economy of Oil?" *Journal of International Affairs* 53, no. 1 (Fall 1999): 6. Morse served as U.S. assistant secretary of state for international energy policy and U.S. representative to IEA.

3. Quoted in Matt Chambers, *Wall Street Journal*, August 27, 2007, R7.

4. Quoted in Simon Henderson, " Al-Qaeda Attack on Abqaiq: The Vulnerability of Saudi Oil," *Policywatch* 1082 (February 28, 2006).

5. Leon Fuerth, "Energy, Homeland and National Security," in *Energy and Security: Toward a New Foreign Policy Strategy*, ed. Jan H. Kalicki and David L. Goldwyn (Baltimore: Johns Hopkins University Press, 2005).

6. "Maritime Security: Public Safety Consequences of a Terrorist Attack on a Tanker Carrying Liquefied Natural Gas Need Clarification" (Washington, D.C.: U.S. Government Accountability Office, GAO 07-316, February 2007).

7. "Guidance on Risk Analysis and Safety Implications of a Large Liquefied Natural Gas (LNG) Spill over Water," Sandia Report SAND2004-6258, Sandia National Laboratories (December 2004), 22.

8. Limited emissions of greenhouse gases are associated with the production of nuclear energy. Fossil fuels are consumed to mine and process uranium, the basis for the fuel of nuclear reactors. However, nuclear reactors themselves do not omit climate-altering gases when operating. Thus, the net emissions of climate-altering gases are quite small.

9. Charles D. Ferguson, "Nuclear Energy: Balancing Risks and Benefits," Special Report 28 (April 2007), Council on Foreign Relations, New York, 16.

10. John P. Holdren, "Commentary on Part VI," in Kalicki and Goldwyn, eds., *Energy and Security*, 554. For an outstanding article on the potential for terrorists to use nuclear energy reactors and programs to receive materials for nuclear weapons programs, see Matthew Bunn and Anthony Wier, "Terrorist Nuclear Weapons Construction: How Difficult?" *Annals of the American Academy of Political and Social Science* 607 (September 2006): 133–49.

11. Sharon Squassoni, "Risks and Realities: The 'New Nuclear Energy Revival,'" *Arms Control Today* 37, no. 4 (May 2007): 6.

12. Squassoni, "Risks and Realities," 11.

Chapter 6. Climate Change

1. Ban Ki-moon, quoted in "UN Council Hits Impasse over Debate on Warming," *New York Times*, April 18, 2007.

2. For an excellent article on the difficulties of collective action to combat climate change, see David G. Victor, "Toward Effective International Cooperation on Climate Change: Numbers, Interests and Institutions," *Global Environmental Politics* 6, no. 3 (2006): 90–103.

3. IPCC, 2007: Summary for Policymakers, in *Climate Change 2007—The Physical Science Basis: Contribution of Working Group I to the Fourth Assessment Report of the Intergovernmental Panel on Climate Change*, ed. Susan Solomon et al. (Cambridge: Cambridge University Press, 2007).

4. Friedemann Mueller, "Energy Security: Demands Imposed on German and European Foreign Policy by a Changed Configuration in the World Energy Market," SWP Research Paper, German Institute for International and Security Affairs (Stiftung Wissenschaft und Politik), RP 2 (English version of SWP-Studie 33/06, January 2007, Berlin), 25.

5. Philip A. Dewhurst, spokesman for Gazprom Marketing & Trading, quoted in Andrew E. Kramer, "Russian Energy Giant to Bundle Carbon Credits with Gas Sales," *New York Times*, April 25, 2007.

6. Ruth Greenspan Bell, "What to Do About Climate Change," *Foreign Affairs* (May/June 2006): 109.

7. David G. Victor, *The Collapse of the Kyoto Protocol and the Struggle to Slow Global Warming* (Princeton, N.J.: Princeton University Press, 2001).

8. Victor, *The Collapse of the Kyoto Protocol*, 47.

9. Interview with John P. Holdren, "The Sky Is Falling," *Bulletin of the Atomic Scientists* (January/February 2007): 45.

10. For more on potential formats for international agreements, see David G. Victor, "Toward Effective International Cooperation on Climate Change: Numbers, Interests and Institutions," *Global Environmental Politics* 6, no. 3 (2006): 90–103.

11. Quoted in Thomas Friedman, "Live Bad, Go Green," *New York Times*, July 8, 2007.

12. Friedman, "Live Bad, Go Green."

Chapter 7. Russia

1. For more on Russia's policies on exports of nuclear energy programs, see Miles A. Pomper, "Russia Looks to Tighten U.S. Nuclear Ties," *Arms Control Today* (November 2006).

2. "From Transition to Development: A Country Economic Memorandum for the Russian Federation," World Bank Report 32308-RU, Washington, D.C., March 2005, 8–9; "Russian Economic Report," no. 7, World Bank, Russia Country Department, February 2004, quoted in Michael Fredholm, *The Russian Energy Strategy and Energy Policy: Pipeline Diplomacy or Mutual Dependence*, (Camberley, Surrey: Conflict Studies Research Centre, Defence Academy of the UK, 2005), 6.

3. "Energeticheskaya strategiya Rossii na period do 2020 goda" (Energy Strategy of Russia to the Year 2020), Government of the Russian Federation Decree 1234-r, August 28, 2003, http://www.minprom.gov.ru/docs/strateg/1; V. V. Putin, "Mineralno-syrevye resursy v strategii razvitiia Rossiiskoi ekonomiki" (Mineral Resources in the Strategy for Development of the Russian Economy),

Zapiski Gornogo Instituta 144 (1999): 3–9, trans. Harley Balzer, "Vladimir Putin's Academic Writings and Russian Natural Resource Policy," *Problems of Post-Communism* 53, no. 1 (January–February 2006): 49–52.

4. *Energeticheskaya strategiya Rossii.*

5. Forty percent of Russia's oil exports flow through the Druzhba pipeline in its two branches. Most of the remaining oil is exported at the Black Sea port of Novorossiysk. A small part is exported using barge and rail traffic.

6. For further discussion of the Druzhba pipeline, see Chapter 3.

7. U.S. Central Intelligence Agency, *The International Energy Situation: Outlook to 1985*, Report ER-77-1624 OU (Washington, D.C.: CIA, April 1977).

8. Putin, "Mineralno-syrevye," 3–9; "Vladimir Putin's Academic Writings," 52.

9. For more on the loans-for-shares policies and the energy oligarchs under Yeltsin, see Marshall I. Goldman, "Putin and the Oligarchs," *Foreign Affairs* (November/December 2004): 33–44.

10. *Christian Science Monitor,* December 28, 2005.

11. "Russia Country Analysis Brief," U.S. Government Energy Information Agency website, http://www.eia.doe.gov/.

12. Putin, "Mineralno-syrevye," 3–9; "Vladimir Putin's Academic Writings," 52.

13. Some of the export of crude by railway is to China to where there is no pipeline infrastructure, thus not an indication of the Transneft bottleneck.

14. "Russia Country Analysis Brief."

15. Putin, "Mineralno-syrevye," 3–9; "Vladimir Putin's Academic Writings," 49–52.

16. "Vladimir Putin's Academic Writings," 51, 53.

17. Juhani Laurila, "Transit Transport Between the European Union and Russia in Light of Russian Geopolitics and Economics," *Emerging Markets Finance and Trade* 39, no. 5 (September–October 2003): 31.

18. "Moscow Issues West a Warning," *International Herald Tribune,* April 7, 2006.

19. Quoted in "Russian Crude Stops Flowing to Europe," *New York Times,* January 8, 2007.

20. RIA-Novosti, June 23, 2004.

21. Laurila, "Transit Transport," 27.

22. "Moscow Issues West a Warning."

23. Laurila, "Transit Transport," 27.

24. *The Economist* (January 7, 2006): 64.

25. "Gazprom Threat to Supplies," *Financial Times,* April 20, 2006, 1.

26. "Belarus Claims Compromise on Oil," *International Herald Tribune,* January 11, 2007, 5.

Chapter 8. Europe

1. "Belarus Claims Compromise on Oil," *International Herald Tribune,* January 11, 2007: 5.

2. Friedemann Mueller, "Energy Security: Demands Imposed on German and European Foreign Policy by a Changed Configuration in the World Energy Market," SWP Research Paper, German Institute for International and Security

Affairs (Stiftung Wissenschaft und Politik), RP 2 (English version of SWP-Studies 33/06, January 2007, Berlin), 5.

3. Mueller, "Energy Security," 7.

4. European Union, "Country Report," Energy Information Agency, U.S. Department of Energy, Washington, D.C., January 2006.

5. "Europe May Ban Imports of Some Biofuel Crops," *New York Times*, January 14, 2008.

6. Commission of the European Communities, "Green Paper: A European Strategy for Sustainable, Competitive, and Security Energy," COM 105, Brussels (March 8, 2006), 17.

7. "Green Paper," 14.

8. "Green Paper," 4.

9. "Green Paper," 14, 16.

10. "Green Paper," 4.

11. "Green Paper,"15.

12. "Green Paper," 17.

13. Quoted in "Russia's Gas Champion Reaches Consumer," *Financial Times*, December 21, 2006.

14. Judy Dempsey, "EU Says Russia Needs to Open Its Gas Pipelines," *International Herald Tribune*, March 31–April 1, 2007, 14.

15. Dempsey, "EU Says Russia," 14.

Chapter 9. United States

1. For U.S. policies on climate change, see Chapter 6.

2. Poll quoted in Michael J. Economides, "The Coming Natural Gas Cartel," www.foreignpolicy.com, March 28, 2006.

3. The ILSA legislation was aimed to address Iran's nuclear weapons program and support for Middle East terror groups. Libya was added to the legislation, though not an initial focus of the initators.

4. State of the Union address, January 2007, http://www.whitehouse.gov/news/releases/2007/01/20070123–2.html.

5. *Washington Post*, quoted in David Deese and Joseph Nye, *Energy and Security* (Cambridge, Mass.: Ballinger, 1981), 5.

6. For ideas in this sphere, see Charles F. Doran, "Life After Easy Oil: A Plan for Escaping the Tightening Noose of Energy Dependency," *American Interest* 3, no. 6 (July/August 2008): 43–52.

Chapter 10. China

1. "China's Energy Conditions and Policies," *People's Daily Online*, December 26, 2007.

2. "China's Energy Conditions."

3. See Chapter 4 for the potential impact the activities of Chinese oil companies may have in countries that the United States sees as security concerns and the effect of those activities on U.S.-Chinese relations.

4. "China," Country Analysis Brief, Energy Information Agency, U.S. Department of Energy, August 2006.

Chapter 11. Iran

1. Theda Skocpol, "Rentier State and Shi'a Islam in the Iranian Revolution," *Theory and Society* 11, no. 3 (May 1982): 265–83.

2. Skocpol, "Rentier State," 280.

3. Iran imports most of its gasoline from the European oil trader Vitol, with 15 percent from refineries in India.

4. Roger Stern, "The Iranian Petroleum Crisis and U.S. National Security," *Proceedings of the National Academy of Sciences* 104, no. 1 (January 2, 2007): 377.

5. A. Q. Khan, founder of Pakistan's nuclear weapons program, ran an illicit nuclear weapons technology operation that sold weapons knowhow to a number of countries, including Iran.

6. See Chapter 4 for a larger discussion of these territorial conflicts.

7. Friedemann Muller, "Energy Security: Demands Imposed on German and European Foreign Policy by a Changed Configuration in the World Energy Market," SWP Research Paper, German Institute for International and Security Affairs (Stiftung Wissenschaft und Politik), RP 2 (English version of SWP-Studies 33/06, January 2007, Berlin), 21.

8. *International Herald Tribune*, February 2, 2007, 1.

Chapter 12. Saudi Arabia and OPEC

1. Edward L. Morse and James Richard, "The Battle for Energy Dominance," *Foreign Affairs* (March/April 2002): 21.

2. For an extensive presentation of this thesis, see Rachel Bronson, *Thicker Than Oil: America's Uneasy Partnership with Saudi Arabia* (New York: Oxford University Press, 2006).

3. Morse and Richard, "The Battle for Energy Dominance," 21.

4. Morse and Richard, "The Battle for Energy Dominance," 20.

5. Morse and Richard, "The Battle for Energy Dominance," 21.

6. Edward L. Morse and Amy Myers Jaffe, "OPEC in Confrontation with Globalization," in *Energy and Security: Toward a New Foreign Policy Strategy*, ed. Jan H. Kalicki and David L. Goldwyn (Baltimore: Johns Hopkins University Press, 2005), 68.

Index

Acknowledgments

This book studies the mutual impact of energy and international relations. Throughout most of its history, international relations theory has placed strong emphasis on geography and material sources of power, such as natural resources. However, in the last quarter of the twentieth century, the interest in the discipline in material power has declined and with it the study of the factor of energy. This book aims to reintegrate the study of energy into key issues of interest in international relations. Hopefully it will be used to incorporate the study of energy into general international relations and political science university courses. The book examines the role of energy in central issues of international relations, such as conflict, stability and interdependency. Through the study of energy in international relations, it aims also to renew interest in the "geo" of geopolitics.

A number of people have made important contributions to *Energy Politics*. First and foremost, I would like to thank Miles Pomper, who has served as an outstanding editor of the manuscript and provided important research insights. I look forward to reading his books in the future. Next, I would like to thank Bill Finan of the University of Pennsylvania Press. Bill nurtured this project through every stage and I am grateful to him for his professional knowledge and beneficial edits. I would like to thank Alison Anderson of University of Pennsylvania Press, who led the production of *Energy Politics*. Thank you to John Gennan for the index and excellent research contributions over the years. I would like to thank Dr. Ed Morse, who has served as an important teacher to me on the dynamics of energy supply. I would like to thank a number of people who have provided important insights into Caspian energy politics: Elin Suleymanov, Galib Mammad, Vafa Quluzade, Temuri Yakobashvili, and Alexander Rondeli. Thanks also to Friedemann Mueller for insights on Europe.